GIVING THANKS:

NEW AND SELECTED POEMS

Also by Tom Hogan

Poems for the Journey

Main Roads and Byways

Texas Dawning

Clouds and Water

Cathedral Rock

The Promise of the Trail Ahead

GIVING THANKS:

NEW AND SELECTED POEMS

TOM HOGAN

*To Garth
a wonderful guy.
Blessings & love
Tom Hogan*

DANCING MOON PRESS
NEWPORT, OREGON

Giving Thanks: New And Selected Poems
copyright © Tom Hogan, 2018
All rights reserved

Without limiting the rights under copyright reserved above, no part of this publication may be reproduced, stored in, or introduced into a retrieval system, or transmitted in any form, or by any means (electronic, mechanical, photocopying, recording, or otherwise) without the prior written permission of the author, except in the case of brief quotations or sample images embedded in critical articles or reviews. The scanning, uploading, and distribution of any part of this book via the Internet, or via any other means, without the permission of the author is illegal and punishable by law. Your support of the author's rights is appreciated. For permission, address your inquiry to: Tom Hogan, tomhogan2@comcast.net

Paperback ISBN: 978-1-945587-25-2
Library of Congress Control Number: 2018908967

Hogan, Tom
Giving Thanks: New And Selected Poems
1. Poetry
I. TITLE

Book editing, design & project production: Carla Perry, Dancing Moon Press
Cover illustration, design & cover production: Sarah Gayle, Sarah Gayle Art
Author photograph:
Manufactured in the United States of America

DANCING MOON PRESS
P.O. Box 832, Newport, OR 97365
541-574-7708
www.dancingmoonpress.com
info@dancingmoonpress.com

FIRST EDITION

Endorsements

In the span of one hundred and twenty-one poems, Tom Hogan covers a lot of geography, both mental and physical. From his obvious love of the Pacific Northwest to travels in Italy, New Zealand, and across America, his poems nearly always reveal a deep spirituality and tenderness toward people—whether familiar or strangers. One can add a self-awareness of vulnerability in the self-effacing humor and irony in some of the pieces, sometimes peeking out from a screen of nostalgia and melancholy. Tom's accounts of the local, the mundane, the quotidian, show a love of place, but not without knowing and drawing its flaws. And humor pervades two of my favorites in this collection: a poem describing a traffic fine in Tuscany, and one implying that the iPhone is the devil himself.

—*Bob Sterry, author of* School of Burglary

Giving Thanks: New and Selected Poems, by poet Tom Hogan represents an impressive body of poetry. Electing to share the empirical, derived from the concourse of his life, the intimate experiences that constitute his being, Tom Hogan gives the reader, the lover of synthesized verse, a volume of poetry that speaks not only to human imagination, but the yearning of the human heart. *Giving Thanks* looks to illuminate what is to be made known to every reader's heart, mind, and yes—soul. The only conclusion a person can draw from this fabulous and voluminous collection is an earnest sense of thanksgiving. *Giving Thanks: New and Selected Poems* is a fine work by Tom Hogan and should be required reading for every serious poet.

—*Emmett Wheatfall*

It is the reader who will give thanks to Tom Hogan for giving the world *Thanksgiving: New and Selected Poems*. The poems offer journeys through different worlds—from the glories of the out of doors, with "jacarandas mixed with oaks," and the "first inkling of blue-black night," to the mysteries of the interior life in which the color yellow "is a mercurial friend," and sounds collect in a "waiting heart." Wherever Tom guides, the reader finds beauty, the result of keen observation and a passionate soul.

—*Greg Chaimov*

Thanksgiving: New and Selected Poems travels many trails, both literal and figurative, each poem rich with voices, history, and appreciation. The title poem, "Thanksgiving," praises squirrel, finch, space heater, black oil, dog poop, hip pain ... all the variety of this life. Reading Tom Hogan, you are in the presence of a pervasive reverence. I am thankful for this book.

—*Penelope Scambly Schott*

Tom Hogan's poems are ones of compassion for all humanity. In these pages, the difficulties faced by a soldier in Iraq and the need of an elderly mother for a ride in the country are of equal concern. This willingness to alleviate suffering finds its roots in both religion and nature. We learn that life "holds us in balance," and contains both "life and decay," thoughts that come on an overnight camping trip. These are, in addition, poems of acceptance and humble gratitude for his own experiences whether beautiful or painful, as is shown in the poem "Thank You." There are questions throughout, one of them leading us to wonder in what ways "Yellow is an attitude." This book is written over decades by a poet now at the height of his powers.

—*Diane Averill*

Giving Thanks is the record of a pilgrim, a seeker engaged in the "hard work" of becoming—day by day, moment by moment—a more appreciative, more compassionate person. In one poem, Tom Hogan asks himself, "How can I be grateful enough?" Time and time again, his poems answer that question. Hogan's collection responds—with piety and humility—to a world in which "It always seems/ like/ we're asked to give more/ than we receive/ until it becomes an act of respect/ and finally love."

—*Paulann Petersen*
Oregon Poet Laureate Emerita

Recognizing that a reliance on yesterday's answers may result in a too-easy certainty, Tom Hogan's poems record and interrogate the world he finds—a world of friendships, family, landscape, promises, memory, public engagement, and private delight. Page by page, Hogan's sense of the sacred and its big questions are never far distant. But it is Tom's patience, his curiosity and keen observation that most strike me. His thoughtfulness and welcome combine to make a large embrace. To open this book is a reader's good luck.

—*Lex Runciman*

Acknowledgements and Gratitude

The poems "Mt. Jefferson Evening," "Drive with Mother" and "The Boat" first appeared in *Synesthesia* at Clackamas Community College; "A Case of Tax Reform" will be appearing in the *Poeming Pigeon*: Vol. 6, In the News.

There have been so many people that helped to make this book possible. I want to thank my first poetry mentor, Diane Averill, for her continual wise support and feedback, and Oregon Poet Laureate Emerita Paulann Petersen for her guidance in the ways of writing and being a poet.

Certainly, I wouldn't have done this without Paul Merchant, who is all kindness. It was he who first made the suggestion for a New and Selected Poems book. His initial encouragement and ongoing support was crucial.

Many thanks Greg Chaimov, Penelope Schott, Paulann Petersen, Lex Runciman, and Diane Averill who read the manuscript and offered valuable ideas and feedback.

Thanks to Elizabeth Miles and Susanna Lungren who proofread the manuscript and caught innumerable errors and made many suggestions, many of which I took.

My Tuesday afternoon poetry group—Susanna, Lundgren, Ron Rasch, Diane Averill, and Helen McNaughton—heard and critiqued the work as it progressed. Thanks much to them. The same is true of my Third Monday Authors group—Elizabeth Miles, Rose Lefevre, Carl Clapp, Kelly Wigmore, and Ron Stone—all heard and reviewed the work as it evolved, and responded with helpful suggestions or kind criticism.

Carla Perry at Dancing Moon Press has been phenomenal.

My lovely wife, Jane Rickenbaugh, who lived through the writing of these and the various trips to get material and put it on paper, deserves high praise. Thanks to her for her grace and love.

Finally, thanks to all who helped with this work and I hope I haven't missed too many of you. I appreciate it.

Contents

Poems For The Journey

Longings 17
Mt. Jefferson Evening 18
Drive With Mother 19
Spring Elements 20
The Organist 21
Idaho Morning 22
Returning From Butte 23
Timothy Lake 24
The Boat 25
Moon Over Lake Gillette 26
Championship Dream 28
Last One Left 29

Main Roads And Byways

Longing II..33
Jefferson Park Winter 34
Exploration 35
Lois The Sister 36
Relearning The Piano 38
The Empty Chair..39
Election Day..40
Mountain Stream Passage 43
Free Association On The Highway 44
San Juan Island Ferry 45

Texas Dawning

Swift Passage 49
Breakfast Griddle Cakes 51
Journey To Bryan, Texas 52
On The Pedernales...54
Two Men With White Cowboy Hats And Friend 57
Z 59
Rotogravure Picture 60
USA Today 62

Clouds And Water
Clouds And Water 67
Preparing For David 68
Albert And The Tuscan Ticket 70
Facing Saint Paul 72
Awake In Assisi 74
Good Friday Walk 76
Holy Saturday 78
Idaho Afternoon Again 79
At The Oceanside 80

Cathedral Rock
Lost 83
Deep Lake 85
South Of Stevens Pass 86
A Faraway Trip 88
A Little Bumpy 90
Blowing In Rome 92
The Aquifer In Magic Valley 93
Fifth Grade At St. Aloysius 96
The Bear Is Power 98

The Promise Of The Trail
Introduction 101
The Promise Of The Trail Ahead: 1-20 102
The Promise Of The Trail Ahead: 21-40 104
The Promise Of The Trail Ahead: 41-50 106

New Poems: I
Listening For Epiphany 109
Poetry 110
My First Connection With Poetry 111
Start Of Another Beautiful Day 113
Janus View 114
My High School English Teacher 116
Birthday 118
To My 24-Year-Old Self 119
Fortune Cookie 120
Things That Happened Since I Heard 121

I'm Not Ready To Be Grateful 123
Accounting 124
First Camp 125
My Cell Phone 126
The Delight Song Of Tom Hogan 127
Lists 128
Time With Maria 129
For Joe 131
Silver Window 132
Asparagus Today 133
Yet To Live 134
A Step Up In Purgatory 135
More To Do 136

New Poems: II
To Be At Cathlamet 141
The Sanctuary 143
Around The Corner 144
East To Orlando 146
Mt. Vernon Morning 147
The Pulpit At The Seaman's Bethel 149
Stagecoach 151
Sunday In Washington, D.C. 152
A Kiwi Voice 153
Counterintuitive Move 154
Milwaukie City Hall 155
At The Track Meet 157
Mother Bear And Her Cub 158
At The Marian Shrine In Orlando 159
Cold Front In Downtown Eugene 161
Desert Corners 162
Oil On The Gulf 163
At The Veterans' Workshop 164
Cold Coffee In Iraq 165
Evening At Bridal Veil 167
On The Pacific Crest Trail 168
Instructions On How To Distinguish A Flower From A Frog 170
Milwaukie Train 171

New Poems: III
Giving Thanks 175
Near Blue Box Pass 177
On Using Words 178
Listening To The Silence 179
I Knew Something Was Wrong 180
I Thought It Was Interesting 181
Arborvitae 182
On The Front Page Of The *New York Times* 183
Brain Surgery 185
Hat And House 187
Reel To Reel 188
Evening Encounter 189
A Case Of Tax Reform 190
Yellow 192
Midnight Mass 193
Time For Biff 195
Hospital Room 196
Gratitude 197
Yellow Bird Is Happy 199
The Invisible Boundary 200
The Oatfield House 201
Facing The Equinox 203
Tree House 204
The Three Essentials 205

About The Author 207

Selected Poems

Poems For The Journey

Chapbook
Privately Printed
(2001)
Portland, Oregon

Longings

I view the darkness before beginning.
Daylight will be here soon.
Minute reflections
glisten in tiny puddles in the street.

My heart is lonely, like a figure in the rain by a lamp post,
alone,
looking,
longing,
waiting for someone or something he doesn't know.

He is like a man in an old black-and-white movie,
post-war Vienna,
or London at night,
lingering for an expected rendezvous.

Being a real man, I am uncertain.
Old answers produce too easily chosen
solutions that fail to satisfy,
like a man who drinks and is still thirsty.
It will be better, I tell myself.
This is only the waiting and the longing.

Mt. Jefferson Evening

Day begins its imperceptible shift to night.
The sun showers on the scarlet hillsides
        in the last vestiges of summer.
We cook on mountain stoves,
        men groping to be close
        and succeeding at companionship.

Dinner is an unforgettable fettuccine Alfredo,
mistakenly made with sweet condensed milk.
        It tastes like some concoction
        balancing precariously
        between delicacy and disaster.
I eat in grateful appreciation.

The night slides swiftly in
        and stars shine bright as diamonds.
Lights speeding across the sky are man-made satellites.
Some go to bed earlier than we ever would at home,
more in rhythm with sun and moon.

Who are we that are so blessed
        with this vista of stars and mountains and trees?
This question seems easier to ask here
        away from the hustle of the flatland.
My fears hover in the foreground,
then fade into the mountainous shadows of the mind
        like a mole finding its hole.

I sit out in the gathering cold listening to the quiet.
Snow will be here soon
        and branches will be clad in a coat of white.
The wind accelerates across the fetch
        and around the tent as the night deepens.
My fingers begin to numb as I try to write.
Darkness surrounds us now
        as the mountain emerges above the moonlight.

Drive With Mother

We drive along the river in the early afternoon.
Easy haze
        hides the direct glare of the sun.
Breezes float along
        carrying summer insects on their appointed rounds.
The river flows gray-green
        as if run through gigantic clothes wringers.
The car
        glides
                along in comforting contentment.
My mother doesn't go out much since eye surgery
        left her sightless in one eye.
Infrequent trips increase their import.
Today the conversation flows
        over relatives and politics.
What was your favorite book?
How did we drive to the mountains?
Did she really call the President that?
Was there any actual news today
        on the talk shows?
She relies now on hearing as eyesight evaporates
        like summer tears.

She fills me in
        on the latest outrages
        with good humor
and a Mark Twain eye for foolishness.
Air cools and comforts.
Traffic moves
        along with us
        in constant motion.
We ride luxuriating in understated companionship.
Lunch remains just
        around the bend.
We'll do this again in the time we have.

Spring Elements

This early spring day I gaze longingly on green
grass growing wild as hibiscus in March downpours.

No brilliant sun today brightens our lives or dries
verdant vegetation. I think of weather vanes

swirling as their yearning drives them through
winter's fulcrum in a hurricane of craving.

These are the days when the infected sky
climbs onto our brow, where each thought

buries itself and enters a world of vapor and
nocturnal stones. The downpour cascades

into a watery vortex and thoughts of gardening
evaporate in the deluge as meaningless and

ineffective as the tractor stationary in the garage,
tires flattened by winter solitude. Oil drips

with a quiet calm from a silent engine,
all awaiting a better day to venture into spring.

THE ORGANIST

For Naomi Perraurd

At evening benediction
the family enters
St. Francis of Assisi Church,
glances at Christ the King on the cross
towering above the altar
in polished maple—
smiling, saintly, ascended—
not like a man in the agony of death.
"You can be like this,"
he seems to say.

Music floats around the wooden pews
from a pump organ
brought by train
from the East in 1895.
Naomi, the parish organist,
lovely and gracious,
elegant in her aloneness,
bends intently
over her keyboard,
creating music underpinning the service.

She plays with that simple grace
belying the artistry
beneath it.
Keys depress,
foot pedals
pump their magic,
the stops coming in orchestrated union
to band the music together
like a framed Rembrandt.

"Holy God, we praise thy name,"
she plays,
pure, sweet,
a honeyed refrain
as the families lift their voices
in thanks and supplication.

Idaho Morning

"Give my love to the world."
Cosmos Mariner *by Conrad Aiken*

One dark morning in Idaho
my feet strike asphalt
running in the creeping cold

as the harvest moon
succumbs to the red-gold
of oncoming day.

What in heaven's name am I doing here?
my legs moan—
it's dark and cold and lonely

as pale breath, exhaled
in ever faster gulps, precedes me,
morning chill covering the fields.

A vehicle crawls out of the dark
then passes in a burst of high-octane energy,
driver surprised to see a solitary runner

as city lights to the south
shine over the waving cornstalks
evidencing life there.

Beyond, a Burlington Northern freight
creeps steadily toward the horizon,
telephone poles thin as toothpicks

behind the engine, emitting whistles
that slowly waft across the fields
marked by pockets of languishing fog.

Waking in the morning Idaho dark,
I reach the day's unfolding destination
by placing one foot after another.

Returning From Butte

The narrow band of blacktop
      arches through the semiarid countryside
like a ribbon on a huge quilt
      continuing to some unseen edge.

Rolling hills replete with sagebrush
      stretch to the horizon.
Water flows from underground aquifers
      creating haphazard lakes

checker-boarded across the landscape.
      A single boat drifts off the nearby island,
the still solitary figure languidly
      beckoning to elusive fish.

Home in Portland is our destination today
      but this road could take us anywhere,
to Tierra del Fuego and back
      like pinballs propelled by a giant plunger.

Green silos sit in staid expectancy;
      a splash of mustard vibrates against the open sky.
Sagging wires   humming with energy
      follow the road into the haze.

A dust devil stirs up the hillside,
      sweeping across fields like a dervish.
The mocking bird dips in swooping staccato,
      while overhead a solitary hawk circles.

How do we know if we are getting close
      when we're not sure where we're going?
"It all depends on where you're trying to get to,"
      the Cheshire Cat said to Alice.

We travel on faith to destinations
      always out of sight,
like St. Paul sailing to Cyprus
      driven by the wind and his vision.

Timothy Lake

Sun shines scarlet in the early morning sky.
Light bounces brilliant off rippling water.
Trees stand tall silent sentinels
over ducks floating on the lake.

I thought you wanted to come here;
it's so beautiful, strange at the same time.
What do we do away from the comforts
of chair and routine of the house?

My father brings out his rod and fly,
casts off in three inches of water,
looking every bit as ridiculous
as a lion tamer with a flyswatter.

How can you teach your son,
when you don't know yourself
the strange depths lurking beneath
the placid surface of pristine Timothy Lake?

The Boat

The boat reclines beached
in the shallows,
yellow grass grown around
its weather-beaten slats.
Grey clouds tumble over one another
to the horizon.
An aura of comfort emanates
from the forgotten hull,
abandoned long ago.
The father had no use for it.

"Where have you been in your life?" I ask.
What have your two faces seen,
stretching Janus-like
in your different worlds?

Travelers sat as you ferried them here and there,
slow or fast, at they wanted,
your topside exposed to boots,
kicks, pushes, a rescuing nail.

Below a different world exists—
watery, teeming,
holding you in balance.
Both bring life and decay.

We floated on you once.
Now there is rest.
No need for putting out to sea today.
You'd still float, with a little love.

Moon Over Lake Gillette

It was the silence, he said,
that stuck out,
silence settling on the home of his youth,
truck farm outside Spokane,
      a county house down the road
surviving amid the city spreading
      out to meet them.

Crickets blanket the lake
      with sound
as the moon continues
      its rise to brilliance in the east,
coming to view, we notice,
through towering electrical wires
      stretching grid-like to the river,
civilization and nature side by side,
      like his home in the Palouse.

A kingfisher or cormorant
circles around and around
      as birds have done
through the growing dusk,
then, suddenly, unexpectedly,
bursts downward from the sky
like a torpedo bomber
slamming into the water
to emerge seconds later,
      dinner in its beak
as it flaps along the wires
toward a perch by the river.

As darkness settles over the lake,
we talk of the world,
      making things right

and what might have been,
the silence always laying up
        to the sound
like pillows in the dark.
We fall into sleep
as the moon rises over misty Lake Gillette.

Championship Dream

I saw long gliding escalators
rising and falling
in the huge open area mall
artificial light in the ceilings
people coming and going
in offhand neutrality
off the "up" escalator I stepped
heading to the Stanley Cup final
Blackhawk logo on my jersey
sharpened skates in bag
plenty of time to get to the arena
I'm sure I knew exactly where it was
In a moment I arrived
at the floating lake on clouds
ice scoreboard nets all in place
no fans in the seats
no coaches no Canadiens no peanut vendors
a team of pee-wee hockey players
took the ice
but I had a trumpet I needed to play
down it fell into the vortex
down I went on the same escalator
down
down again
but no trumpet could be found
abandoned this search
back up the escalators
high-rising glass walls to the ceiling
my high school friend emerged
from the locker room
I saw him
knew I was in the wrong rink
the stadium was across town

Last One Left

I never thought I'd be the only one left,
        my mother used to say
when talking about her life,

her mother dying in a nursing home,
my father four years after his first stroke,
her brothers and sisters all gone,
as well as the Grey girls
        who lived down the country road
        toward Granger in the Yakima Valley.

I never knew them,
        only heard her talk about them,
and I used to wonder why it was so hard—
she had her books, and her radio,
she was alive
and lucid until the day she died.

I used to wonder about that
until my friends started leaving:
        Warren, my Italian compatriot,
        and John Entwhistle of The Who,
Naomi, the organist at church,
Carroll O'Connor,
and Sister Clare, cremated when I didn't know
we could do that,
Charlie, ten years younger,
on whom we shoveled dirt at the cemetery.

I used to wonder
        until I started to feel superfluous,
as if time was passing me by.
The kids seemed younger and younger,
computers were now everywhere

      like hatched omnivores
and we can talk only to automated machines,
      no real people there.

Things aren't the way they should be anymore.
And I think about my mother,
being the last one.

Main Roads and Byways

Chapbook
privately printed
(2005)
Portland, Oregon

Longing II

The woman reclining on her deck gazes at the lake.
The red robin chirps unnoticed on the branches above.
The earthworm ducks behind the dirt clump.
The green maple leaf sadly stares at his brown coat.

The book aches on its shelf third down from the top.
The calendar waits in purgatory for a new year.
The pencil in the red teacup yearns to shake its dust.
The fountain pen full of ink sprawls on the desktop.

The foreman works at his desk surveying the sunlight.
The black coffee splashes over the book of poetry.
The picture lies alone outside the bright photograph album.
The water laps against the dock waiting for a swimmer.

The policewoman pulls a glove over her trigger finger.
The burglar wishes he had brought his lock-picking tools.
The motorcycle on the hoist yearns for a mechanic.
The Lotus driver hungers for the freedom of the green light.

Jefferson Park Winter

The deer skips across the half-frozen stream
eyeing greener leaves on the far side.
A hawk glides over the terrain,
a solitary sentinel seeking his daily meal.

The lakes shimmer in the declining
afternoon sun as silence reigns.
Squirrels and chipmunks scurry tirelessly about
searching for unclaimed nuts and cones

as I emerge up the trail out of the woods
to the always-thrilling Jefferson Park vista,
hidden lakes half-shrouded in mist
lying as if in a huge rocky jewel box.

Fall colors fade in the first breath of winter.
Storm clouds swirl suddenly around the mountain
blotting out the sun and dropping the temperature
precipitously. The lakes lie now in shadow.

In hotter days dinosaurs roamed this park.
A brontosaurus stood ankle-deep in water, chewing
tropical leaves. Wolves and woolly mammoths,
with their upward curved tusks, came with the ice.

Finally came man, first to establish a toehold,
then to survive, then to dominate.
I try to exist in harmony with the savage beauty
and grace of the park as windy night settles in.

Exploration

with Ron Rasch

"We shall not cease from exploring
And the end of all our exploring
Will be to arrive where we started
And know the place for the first time."
—T. S. Eliot

As the moon within
    circles the earth reborn,
the ancient tide of stars
    appears still, yet soaring.

Vivid is the path lighted
    by these celestial bodies
like a hallway in some
    German expressionist movie,
guiding me toward a forgotten destination.

To the very degree of
    strangeness, the German
journey clarified the familiar—
    as a train jostling through
centuries of angst, arrived
as at a Valhalla
    of selfhood,

our exploration ending,
    yet beginning
peace achieved in standing still.

Lois The Sister

I

Today I drive down the hill
      to the river
looking for Lois, the lost sister,
      fall rain pelting the windshield,
murky clouds hovering the horizon.

I remember Naomi, her sister,
      the organist of my youth,
four years gone now,
leaving Lois alone,
      defenseless,
the house empty of music,
      laughter,
      conversation,
not even important conversation but any conversation

Lois knew Naomi's death was coming
      but still was unprepared,
this catastrophe of life
      hitting her
like a twenty-foot tsunami.

At Naomi's funeral,
      I had promised Lois
      a poem about Naomi,
      wrote it actually six months later.
Then, whenever I saw Lois,
I looked into her vacant eyes
      unable to say anything,
guilt piling up in my liver.
One day I put the poem in my book,
      unseen by Lois.

II

The time arrived to fix that failure
        but I had lost Lois.
She didn't come to church anymore;
        she wasn't at home either.
        No one knew where she was.
One person said she'd died,
        another that she was in a nursing home.
Finally Ann, the parish secretary,
        produced an address.
"It's a rest home," she said,
        "somewhere like that."

The dead-end street levels out
        at the bottom of the hill,
the river flows swiftly now
        past the houses
        on the river bank,
no nursing home there.
No one knows anything
        about anyone named Lois.
I have to turn to the work of the day.

Tomorrow is another day
        to find out
        if she's there,
        at a nursing home by the river—
and if she's there,
if her mind's still there.
Even if she can't understand,
I can still read the poem
        to pay some lingering debt.

Relearning The Piano

The black-and-white keys stare up at me,
        reveling
                in their solidity,
daring the unprepared to play,
        welcoming the virtuoso.
Each ivory stands clear and exact
        in Sphinx-like silence,
energy waiting to be released.

I have lived with an authentic piano
        for decades,
her player cousin only a distant memory.
She's been a member of the family,
        but playing
                has been for others
since I won that now-hollow victory
        to escape her serpentine clutches.
Dust settled on her keys.

How did I get here?
        What do I have to do?
Practice and more practice,
        comes the dreaded answer.
You have to play yourself.

Mozart heard symphonies in his head
        but still needed practice.
The piano remains in her regal repose.
I bring the music with me as I approach.

The Empty Chair

The old wooden chair
        sits upright,
quiet in the darkness of early evening.
The boy gazes at it from the dining room table
        after dinner,

wondering if someone is sitting there.
Why can't I see you?
Why don't you show yourself?

There must be more to you
hiding among the reeds
        than baseball statistics
        and bridge bidding.
No need to explain, you insinuate
and others must go along with you.

How is one to learn
        the way to do things
if you don't tell how it is?
How does one find the
        slippery handle?

Where is that deep person
        that resides in the psyche,
who knows things,
goes to the core?

I look, trying to find you
        and, failing that,
believe I'm failing myself.
The chair continues its subtle rocking.

Election Day

I
Ireland—1770

Verdant fields lie fallow in once-plowed ground.
Rain beats down on clover and men and
grass sprouts between roof thatches.
Sheep graze over mossy rock piles.
A starving dog watches the scene with eyes
      dead as oysters.

The country road stretches through abandoned farms where
children shun half-rotten potatoes.
Where has all the food gone?
Onto ships, they say, bound for Cherbourg, Calais
      and Copenhagen.
In Dublin, men in wigs converse over tea, a roaring fire
      warming them.

In London, the King converses in German about benign neglect
while speakers in Parliament debate the naval question.
Members buy and sell seats without the inconvenience of
election and make policy for unprotected provinces.
The Duchess of Marlborough's ball is the highlight
      of the Season.

The landless farmer stares at the board in the
now-deserted church.
Rain pours through the tatters in his wife's shawl and
they stare expectantly.
The broadside cries the beauty of America;
      if only they could read.

I ache for my ancestors.

II
Nicaragua—1957

The sun bears down on the parched ground.
A lizard scampers across the porch.
Out in the yard, a colony of ants feast on a dying scorpion.

A boy stares at the boarded-up windows.
Two soldiers in camouflage gear stand guard authoritatively,
submachine guns resting nonchalantly in their young hands.

No one knows exactly what has happened.
There was an announcement on the radio and
rumors flow like electric current along invisible wires.

Children watch warily from nearby doors.
A couple approach, then turn and walk away.
Dogs hurry about their daily business.

"Maybe they'll be coming," the guards say.
There will be no election today.
There's been a change at the capital.

I ache for my neighbors.

III
Portland—November 9, 2002

Rain bears down the branches on this damp election day.
Yellow leaves adorn the ground in the early morning.
The Election Station shows scant signs of life as
I slide into my post in the dark, placard in hand.

I see my breath in the damp air
as gray sunlight begins to chase away the night.
A single figure approaches, silently entering the school.
A second voter wonders if I should be there.

The morning solitude continues unabated.
Teachers cart their day's lessons in over-stuffed cases.
Children begin arriving on yellow school buses,
more curious than their elders.

A couple gingerly exit their car, notes in hand.
A man stops to talk—"She's going to win," he says.
Classes commence and the street continues deserted.
Where are the others who should be coming?

The business manger didn't have time to register.
The garbage man didn't have time to vote.
The stockbroker sits hoping for a market upswing as
anxious shoppers begin to fill the malls.

Nothing remains to complete here.
My coffee is cold and numbed fingers pack signs.
Other locations may hold more promise.
Still, this is better than a coup.

I ache for my country.

Mountain Stream Passage

The bridge over Carbon Creek washed out—
only two spindly logs offer precarious
passage this afternoon across the dark

torrent cascading off Carbon Glacier.
It would have been safer in the morning;
I ruminate in sun-baked silence on the

north bank, tears welling up suddenly,
a mountain pica nodding agreement.
I notice the fields of purple heather

all around with orange-red splashes
embroidering this imperial cloak.
Gray rocky runoff rushes in front

of me down the mountain stream bed,
snow-covered Mt. Adams above,
craggy, silent, holding its fire

beneath its elegant white topcoat
to erupt someday on its own time.
A fall off the pencil-thin logs

could break my legs, sweep my pack
down the mountain. If fording, I would
be wet yet again, the current running

swiftly enough to knock down a deer,
threatening to suck anything under
its pounding glacial torrent, this

bridge wash-out forcing a wade-across.
I do it because I have to, like other decisions.
I wade into the swirling water.

Free Association On The Highway

Clouds hover over sagebrush,
far downriver,
no purple riders in sight.

Hills usually brown retain
the surprising chartreuse of spring,
like oblong billiard balls in the distance.

A tendril of bridge crosses
the Columbia River, like a metallic
ribbon on a deep-blue quilt.

Cars glide past at dizzying speeds.
Where are the state police
when you need them?

We drink coffee,
thinking of Albert Einstein.
Is everything really relative?

Music plays silently
in ragged glory
in the motel rooms of our minds.

Atonement emerges,
like a lazy rider out of desert mirage,
giant orange sun behind.

San Juan Island Ferry

Darkness lies on the water like a huge
        down quilt, a single red
bulb illuminates the ferry landing

as water laps continuously at pilings
        sliding darkly
into the murky sound. On the beach

the heron stands at attention, neck
        darting intermittently
into water in search of an unsuspecting meal.

The four-story ferry hums quietly connected
        to the terminal as we
drive into its cavernous bottom deck. Above

we walk onto decks blazing with long rows of
        oversized tables lining
sides and center. A lady receives a paper note

from her husband, a Mona Lisa smile flickering
        in her eyes. Passengers
choose coffee and muffins from the cafeteria, mothers

watch children near an inexplicable red danger tape
        we easily duck under. Suddenly
the engines hum into action. Just on time the

brigantine ferry begins to slide effortlessly from
        the terminal, so smooth the dock
itself looks as if it were moving. The ship's wake

makes it clear we're sailing. A white seagull
    swoops to perch on the rail.
The ferry moves ever faster across the

wine dark sea, like Odysseus' swift blue ships
    carrying passengers and crew
into the starry night, the next dock just out of sight.

TEXAS DAWNING

CHAPBOOK
FIR TREE PRESS
(2006)
CLACKAMAS COMMUNITY
COLLEGE
OREGON CITY, OREGON

Swift Passage

I

Blue-green lakes lie
        as plentiful as marbles
dotting the landscape below my 737.
Ice still sits on bone-chilling water
        even at 2:45 in the afternoon
with sun beaming down.
Brown fields in squares and
        rectangles reside domino-like
with pine trees budless
        in the late Minnesota winter.
Four days ago, it was snowing here
        and white remnants remain
to remind me, looking down
        god-like
From my high perch
that winter still sits hard on the land.

II

Green and brown rolling hills smooth
        through the southwest countryside.
Bluebonnets, Indian paintbrush
        and lupine line the highways,
red and yellow and blue
        showing spring now
        and summer to come.
The brownish-gray water
flows toward the gulf
with mesquite bushes pushing
their stickly arms
into adventuresome gringos

and jacarandas mixed with oaks
greening the fields dotted
      with puffs of cow pats
marking the steers' passage.
Hawks floating on air
      soar below waiting for lunch.
The land here readies for summer
two hours from ice.
We get ready for re-entry,
begin our descent to Austin.

Breakfast Griddle Cakes

Baking in the morning Texas sun,
we stop at Mo's roadside diner,
two wrecked '60 Chevys out back
and sagebrush stretching down
the road to the horizon line.

"Let's get some breakfast fixings,"
my friend says, buckwheat cakes
hot off the griddle or spiced catfish and grits
like his mother served at their home
up the road across the county line.

Brown sugar shakers stand silent sentinel
on the counter, guarding the rising
of these morning pancakes and Texas sausage
on the red-hot griddle as the first tiny bubbles
perk up through the moist yellow batter.

A hawk soars outside the window
and dips down to the bluebonnets,
just missing a scurrying brown pica
scrambling to safety down its hole.
Our breakfasts arrive from the griddle.

We hear about sharecropping
in the 1950s, growing up black and poor,
picking cotton in 110-degree afternoons,
the breakfast fixings feeding our bodies
as the words fill our souls.

Journey To Bryan, Texas

Today four concrete ribbons
stretch forward to the sight line.
Rolling hills undulate
across purple sagebrush and
green scrub trees spring up
across this low mid-Texas hill country.

A small white Baptist church
sits silently by the roadside, grass
uncut for weeks, a cemetery attached
with unattended gravestones, an ancient
picket fence long in need of some saving
paint, slouching around the grounds.

Cattle graze in fields everywhere,
ready for market to feed the city folks
in Pecos Chuck Wagons and McDonalds.
Red paintbrush, called Texans, they tell me,
nestle with the purple bluebonnets
growing in the median and alongside the road.

This seems to be the American heartland
of small farms and lazy countryside
far removed from the urban hustle of
too much traffic, too many people,
interchangeable buildings, and gas
stations lacking jacks to change a tire.

We pull into a small Texas town
with old brick buildings and facades
from *The Last Picture Show*,
a gas station with a flying red Mobil
horse sign seldom seen in any
urban center since World War II.

"I was born over there,"
my friend Clyde says.
"The white people
lived up in College Station,
near Texas A & M.
We lived down here."

On The Pedernales

Orange Indian paintbrush grows
      in the green fields
and oak trees dot the landscape,
seventh graders from Trinity Lutheran
      in Fort Worth
      crowd onto the bus,
bluebonnets lie everywhere,
      the air clear,
      water muddy,
and wildflowers flash in the sun.

Yellow school buses take us around
      to see LBJ's ranch.
Born in 1908,
he was a Representative at 28,
living on this Perdernales River,
      flowing through the land
      they call
      the Texas Hill Country,
a man nurtured by the land
      in some way
      I don't exactly understand.
We drive along the Perdernales.
I never thought I'd be here
listening to "Blowin' in the Wind"
      in 1966,
seeing the wars on TV,
      explosions in the jungle
and a little naked girl
      running down the road
      covered in napalm.

Today
      I see more

with the vision of history,
400-year-old oak trees,
balls of air moss on the limbs,
and the big house
      on the river facing the river
      22 bedrooms,
      78 telephones,
a Monarch butterfly drifting
      across the lawn
and water tanks half-filled
      with rainwater,
a 650-year-old oak tree,
      and green mistletoe
      in the mesquite trees,
rolling hills all around.

I know I'd feel
      comfort out here
as he did,
away from the city life
      that we chose:
he never really left for good,
producing
a "better and balanced viewpoint"
      as he said.

I recall the good that he did:
      education for everybody
      the Water Quality Act
      Medicare
Endangered Species Act
      freedom of opportunity for all
      Head Start
      National Endowment for the Arts

        Public Broadcasting
        Civil Rights Act
        Voting Rights Act
        National Historical Places Act
and 200 others I overlooked
        while condemning his
        Texas manner
        and Vietnam mistake.

Green cacti grow all around
        and black Indian antelope
stand among the trees,
a three-month-old fawn
        races back and forth
        with graceful abandon.
Hawks glide
        over the treetops.
It always seems
        as though
we're asked to give more
        than we receive
until it becomes an act of respect
and finally love.

He was a big man
        six-foot-four
with a grin
and endless opinions coming at you
energy
and a home on the Pedernales
but lost without his Ladybird.

Two Men With White Cowboy Hats And Friend

Today in the dawning Texas sun
they stood just outside the wooden frame door
wearing white cowboy hats.

One, black-skinned, had brought his
from the green rain country,
the other, white-skinned, bought his
at Walmart
the way real Texas cowboys do.

Their friend wanted one, maybe,
because Tom Mix had one,
but he never wore
      his white cruise cap
      or black student beret
      or any other hat
      but old ones he'd earned running races.
He knew he'd never wear it,
so passed this time.

You weren't sure from the photograph
why they came
but it seemed to be some sort of search
pushing them on to this destination
for a better sense of roots, maybe,
hearts linked by some invisible elliptical arc

that helped them to try to maintain
that reservoir of good
the former President, their object,
seemed to maintain
above all his flaws.

You could see it in their eyes, shining
in the morning Texas dawn,
their faces reflected in the telephoto lens,
a hawk floating above
as the sun sprung above the motel roof.

Z

"Write a poem about Texas," he said.
"You could do that while we're talking,"

and I thought I could or should
or maybe I ought to do something

that homages the red and orange
in the waitresses' shirts serving us

spicy foods, no Texas accents here, only
one or two we've heard in the entire time.

"It's all changed," the waiter said,
a fact of life to which we pay lip service

but disconcerting when we're in the midst
of facing an unknown future or death.

The 1960s movie, Z, rose from my memory,
a documentary about a putrid Greek scandal:

Yves Montand assassinated by thugs,
students painting Zs on the pavement

—in ancient Greek, "He lives still"—
while being beaten by police in uniform.

Z used to be a Greek political scandal;
now it's a restaurant in Austin, Texas.

Rotogravure Picture

Who are the people
        in the old-style picture
as they look
into the camera
        and into my life?

Can they see me
        as well
        as I can see them,
sitting on the farmhouse porch
        in Blanco County, Texas,
circa 1898,
cornhusks lying
        beside the house,
        sagebrush under the porch?

The picture speaks
        as if it was today.
Two men wear ties,
        out of step with the rest
who have shirt collars
        buttoned around their necks.

Are they all dead now?
What were their lives like?
Did he achieve his dream?
She her marriage?
        How did it turn out?
        Where are they all going?
What is there to do?
Did they vote for Teddy Roosevelt?

Times are different;
people are the same.
      Their spirits remain,
staring out their picture window
as I sit in the county library,
Blanco County
circa 2006.

USA Today

I watch a beautiful flight attendant prepare
packaged meals and drinks as our plane
bounces along against headwinds
of eighty pounds per square inch.

White and yellow garbage bags line the aisle
as pale ale flows to the couple across,
vodka with a twist to a striped-shirted man,
a small diet soda over ice for me.

USA Today says soldiers stop to rescue
a woman with a baby shot on a bridge;
the *New York Times* reports that the soldiers
shot her "accidentally" as she fled the scene.

The byline column reports the Secretary
of Defense saying solemnly, "We'll make
every effort to keep the unavoidable civilian
casualties to the absolute minimum possible,"

while baseball welcomes the new season
with a snowstorm in Baltimore. A woman
from first class struts the aisle
in a flaming red sweater, while the captain

tells us all to "sit back and enjoy the service."
My seatmate reads his *USA Today*,
while an hour ago we heard about some
mysterious new respiratory disease arriving

on a plane from Hong Kong, like a standby
extra passenger. Waiting travelers watched
the news as if they knew it was important,
as citizens of Hippo in St. Augustine's

time watched the Vandals arriving at the gates
going about their daily business,
debating about the nature of the Trinity
until the barbarian troops were in the city.

Clouds and Water

Chapbook
Fir Tree Press
(2007)
Clackamas Community College
Oregon City, Oregon

Clouds And Water

White clouds
out the window
brown fields passing below
crossing America's heartland.
We fly.

Black man
standing silent
sentinel observing
Texas chef flipping pancakes.
We eat.

Green grass
over water
oozing up from the deep
giving hope to lives in need.
We grow.

Preparing For David

I remember the first time I saw him
        32 years ago.
My first instinct was:
    I'm glad I'm not a sculptor.
What would anyone produce after him?
What ego would try?

Today I lean again against the
        marble wall
        waiting,
preparing
        to see him again,
        procrastinating,
        overwhelmed.

The "Prisoners" still stand guard
        all along the hall,
struggling mightily
        to free themselves
        from their stone blocks,
to stand like him.

My lip begins to quiver just a trifle,
not so much that anyone can see.
What have I accomplished
        since I was here last,
        all that time ago?
Achievements, yes,
        but nothing like this titan.

Light shines from above,
radiates up from below,
olive benches lean against the walls.
To my left stands a guard,

      sweating,
      hungry for his next cigarette,
      his pot belly hanging over his pants,
      his belt the same size as his youth.
      It sags to his skinny hips.
He is with David six days a week
      but yearns for his wife, his pasta
      and *vino rosso extraordinaire.*

An olive frieze circles the ceiling,
the floor made of sandstone tiles,
all dwarfed by the statue
      breathing in the distance.
What will there be to do after something like this?

Michelangelo had other commissions,
      chiseled other statues.
The importance of any honest achievement
seems to diminish
when confronted by this physical reality
      looming past the "Prisoners."
What is important
      and how do we decide?
I ask, as I begin the walk down the hall
      toward David.

Albert And The Tuscan Ticket

I

He stands, muscled and expectant,
before the Luccan magistrate,
pensive behind his mahogany desk.
The orange Tuscan sun bakes

the red roof tiles and beats through
the windows opening onto the piazza.
The officer gazes so thoughtfully at
the documents spread before him.

"He is sorry," he says, "very sorry."
They are all sorry, very sorry,
but there is nothing they can do as
the bougainvillea perspires outside.

His car was parked in a pedestrian lane
and the ticket and fine are unfortunately in order.
Other officers enter to consult with the magistrate,
Italians in uniforms with white sashes,

blue short-sleeved shirts, blue hats,
creases in their dark blue pants,
automatic pistols in white buttoned holsters,
medals adorning chests of all but one.

They are all sorry, very sorry,
they would do something if they could,
but it is totally out of their hands.
Mr. Albert, unfortunately, will have to pay.

II

He didn't have to go and we all knew that.
He talked about what would happen
if he just left the country and how ever
would they know. They don't follow up

on anything in the whole country
except art, food, women, and the Pope.
He told us they were all very sorry
but he still had to pay his 68 Euros.

"It was like a sexual experience," he'd say later.
"You pay your money and you get your screwing."
Irony covered his pain and uncertainty in this.
He was sorry and they all were very sorry

but I was happy for him, expecting no less,
really, from my friend, Albert, who once rode his bicycle
down the Pacific Coast 1100 miles to San Diego.
He had that day stood before the Tuscan magistrate

and emerged like Sir Gawain from his encounter
with the Green Knight, scathed, wiser, poorer,
but alive, richer in spirit, a coating of irony painted
on his recounting of this remarkable adventure.

Facing Saint Paul

Green cypress trees laze against the church,
a little girl chases her yellow balloon past
green park benches while the Roma buses
belch exhaust fumes across the Via Paulina.

My lip trembles as I linger outside under
the cypress trees in the basilica park, watching
schoolgirls buy ice cream cones. A blue bird
sits uninterested on a nearby branch.

I gape at the statue of St. Paul, fourteen feet
tall, sword and Bible in hand, fierce
to give the word of God to the whole world.
"Here is your call," he seems to be saying.

"To preach! To talk! To minister!"
There are no words yet from my mouth.
I want to avoid all this, but the emotion
continues throughout mass. I cry

during most of it. The balding Italian priest
who reads his sermon in a monotone,
believing what he says, doesn't seem to
lose his listeners but doesn't block my tears.

He shows his fervor in the way he holds up
the host and the chalice for all to see,
his open arms giving peace. He believes.
Nuns in orange and black-flowered blouses
kneel opposite our pew, fingering rosaries.
A lady in a purple dress fans herself, while
the daily lector in white shirt and pants
crosses himself before reading the epistle.

Paul burned for God, truth and salvation,
received his commission and carried it out.
I tear again as I write about it. My defenses
against the message lie embedded deep,

giving me busy work, getting me off track,
drifting into Calypso's siren songs.
I find it hard to answer this call of Paul,
to utter out loud statements like:

"Salvation is for everyone."
"Put on the armor of God."
"Defend yourself against evil
In heavenly places."

To run the good race for salvation
seems what's asked at St. Paul
Outside the Walls. Devotion seeps
from the very stones in the basilica,

down the aisles, out the mosaics
overhead. Two rows of Roman columns
lead to the exit. St. Paul's eyes bore into
my back as I walk to the bus on the corner.

Awake In Assisi

A rusty moon glistens watchfully
over the brown Umbrian morning.

Cool breezes filter through our window,
shutters opened to admit Assisi.

Beige mourning doves chirp the sun up;
a red glow lies low in the eastern sky.

Ashen clouds show the hint of a light gray,
morning haze hovering over a darker hue.

Sepia buildings line the street,
riveted rocks restraining the roof tiles.

I woke last night to a dog barking
at an unperturbed cat street-walking.

Eight hundred years ago, before there
was a basilica, before anything grand,

St. Francis labored here. Mass is in an hour
and I have premonitions, of what I don't know.

The place exudes low-key spirituality, this
morning more satisfying than the shopping

that filled our hours and minds yesterday.
I don't know what I expected here,

a message maybe, like the one Paul received
on the Damascus road. That would at least

be clear. Today I'm awake, Mass is in an
hour and I'm allowed to make up a Sunday.

I seem to be peaceful about that,
not yet afraid of facing Paul in Rome.

Maybe there's nothing new here,
maybe I already know what the call is,

the message emerging in quiet little tunes.
The bird's song diminishes as morning develops.

I see green now on the valley below,
the moon sleeps in the clouds.

Morning has arrived in the Umbrian hills
as this pilgrim has awakened in Assisi.

Good Friday Walk

Sun's rays gliding through my bedroom window
trumpet a beautiful spring day. No rain beats
on the body or spirit. Dew glistens on the new grass

like tiny light bulbs softly surrounding their green
filaments, frost lingering from the night chill of the
second blue moon since 1915 in a single year. I am

star-struck in amazement at the times in which I live.
The day seems very much like the one when you
walked your road to crucifixion, driven hard

by that same cruelty and hatred that thrives today
in Uganda and Darfur and Sudan and down the street.
Did you have time to glimpse that moon while

sweating blood as others slept? No clouds would
have been in the sky over Jerusalem to mar the view.
Taunting voices rang out from the dark as you were led

here, then there, by elders so eager to condemn, they called
themselves out of bed in early dawn. Did you have any
time to see the bright bougainvillea as you were led along

the hot dusty road, wood on your back, your body
beaten black and bloody? Yet you fell only three times
the whole way, reminding me of my daily slip-sliding

with less to carry. The scratch on my foot aches with a
single sliver needing extraction as I shiver, envisioning
nails being driven into your pulpy flesh. Did you know

the sun's beauty as death approached there on the hill,
only a mother and a few friends remaining until
the end? I don't believe you had those luxuries

as I talk to a friend, pick up our lawn tractor and prepare
a meal, pray in the early morning cool. I'm thankful
to be able to walk along with you on this good day.

Holy Saturday

Today I arrive for church on Holy Saturday,
the service uncomfortably early as in
older days, only a faithful few attending,

just like the scene we celebrate. Jesus is dead
and in the tomb. Peter and John, even Magdalene,
are desolate. He is dead and it is done.

Despair rolls in like billowing clouds,
turmoil spreading its oily fingers
engulfing everything within its reach.

"What do you want from me?" I ask.
"Wait and cherish," comes the response
as if whispered at some barely audible level.

Rain beats on the car roofs outside.
Summer awaits the passing days.
Easter is close upon us tomorrow.

Idaho Afternoon Again

I run the road again today
in the Ascension Priory triangle,
pavement stretching uphill
to the far distant sightline,
yellow line in the middle,
jogging the Idaho afternoon
with a limp the body says
repeatedly, "Pay attention to me."

I don't know if I can finish this
as a blue Oldsmobile whizzes by
with its muffler spewing grey smoke.
I glance across the brown fields
bare of sugar beets and alfalfa and wheat,
down the hill across the vacant railroad
tracks, with the light of Twin Falls across
the winding distant Snake River Canyon.

A hint of pain gurgles in my hip, bone
scrunching in a socket bare of cartilage.
Sweat begins to drip down my arms
and my lungs ache for oxygen
in the 4400-foot sagebrush altitude
far above the comfortable 50 feet at home.
My body leans over and over into the road
pushing through maybe one more time.

At The Oceanside

Morning sun slides
        over the landward hill line.
A brown speckled gull saunters past
        sandy driftwood.

People far down the beach
        cut figures like tiny black dots
and Cape Lookout looms
        beyond the tranquil bay,

hidden in the morning haze,
        its craggy line
seeming a cardboard cutout
        against the misty vapors behind.

A cloudbank hangs out to sea,
        maybe four hours distant,
beckoning afternoon rain to drive
        the sun into hibernation.

Yesterday was glorious,
        walking the beach,
running into the wind,
        soaking up the Saturday sun.

This morning gliding down the hill
        and up again against the grain
felt strangely easier than expected,
        the distance closer than the eye.

White capped waves undulate
        onto the beach in their rhythmic pattern,
a dog chases an orange ball
        thrown with the wind down the beach.

I walk along.

Cathedral Rock

Chapbook
Fir Tree Press
(2008)
Clackamas Community College
Oregon City, Oregon

Lost

"Be patient to all that is unsolved in your hearts/
and try to love the questions themselves."
—Rainer Maria Rilke

My poem was lost.
The fact dawned on me like hot whips of panic.
Now I faced the blank white page.

I wrote it last Friday on a napkin
in the white Red Cross tent in Vernonia
while eating lunch elbow to elbow

with seventy-six other tired disaster responders.
We ate ham and cheese, mustard, full-fat
chips and mayo, cookies if you wanted.

"This is better than our school lunches,"
the high school senior said sitting across
the table in his torn blue jeans and white tee shirt.

We could see the brown water line
four feet up the Century Market across the street
and just at the roof of the medical clinic next door.

Three women and a child with glazed eyes
approached the food counter apologetically
with their savage loss seeping into our gut.

That's why we were here. Our good
fortune sat today on my shoulders like
some reprehensible weight. Is everybody lost

or do some just look that way? I felt like
a taxi driver gliding through Times Square
past the silent neon glare reflected everywhere.

I can replace my poem, I thought.
They will have to replace their dreams.
We drove down the hill out of Vernonia.

Deep Lake

Close to dusk
at last I have a quiet time to
    write
sitting around the camp
as the shadows lengthen,
Steve and his brother Sam out
    for a walk
around the lake basin.

Seamus Heaney's, *The Spirit Level*
    lies on my knee.
He writes about
    getting a quiet time.
I've been so busy
    so much
      it seems hard

to breathe every so often.
I dug deep
    yesterday
pulling up the last climb
and said it was the altitude.
Maybe it was,
    as I see the blue-green water

and snow up on the cliff tops,
a raven swirling down to water's edge
and thin white rivulets
    cascading into the lake.

The slender volume of poetry
    speaks
a kept promise.
I will write the book if it's important.
Maybe it's not the altitude.

South Of Stevens Pass

Steve saw the squirrel.
It ran past the evergreens with a nut in its mouth.
Steve was tired. It had rained all night
and he was wet too.
He wondered why he was here.
Was it a search for meaning in this chaotic world?
He didn't ask that question yet today.

Steve's friend was tired too.
His toes hurt since he stubbed
them on a rock yesterday morning.
His pack was heavy.
They were far behind their other two friends.
He talked to Steve in front.
"I wonder how Hemingway would describe this hike.
He had a great style.
Faulkner drank.
He wrote a little, too, between bottles."

Steve watched the trail ahead.
Rain fell on his hat brim.
He saw it run down his walking stick.
Is this the way of life? he thought.
He didn't know.
He'd leave that up to his friend lagging behind.
Tom was always talking about something or other.

Steve knew only that he beat cancer.
He could hike now, when he thought
It was impossible a year and a half ago
lying in his hospital bed.
It was sterile there in the ward.
Now he saw the trees.
It was green here in the North Cascades.

Where was he going?
At least to the end of the trail, he knew.
What was the meaning?
He didn't know.
They walked on and the rain beat down.

A Faraway Trip

Delia thought she'd had that dream before.
      She stood quite still on the porch today
looking at the marmot whizzing around
the few blades of grass still remaining
      on this slow Louisiana August day.

Swimming was out of the question.
      She looked across the road
down the bayou with its eucalyptus
branches hanging down to the greenish water.
She saw the yellow signpost
      with the symbol of an alligator
above the words "no swimming."
No one is swimming, she thought.

She'd dreamed last night of the mountains
      in the Northwest with their Douglas firs
and alpine lakes reposing
in the glacier-cut troughs.
      There were celestial passes for the trails.
Mrs. Robicheaux had talked about them in
      geography class yesterday.
There was even a trail, she'd said, all the way from
      Canada to Mexico, called the Pacific Crest Tail
or some such thing.

That was probably why she'd had the dream.
She saw hikers carrying packs on their backs
and walking up one hill and down the other side.
They carried tents and gear she'd never
      even heard of before.
And how sweaty and tired they all seemed.
One walked with a decided limp
      as if his hip hurt

or maybe he had blisters on his toes, she didn't
know. Another had a bag from some operation.
It was raining, too, and they were wet
        but they didn't seem to mind—
They seemed to be doing it by choice,
        for fun even.

She didn't understand that.
She'd never been anywhere really
        except to New Orleans once,
before the big storm a year and a half ago.
She'd loved going down Canal Street
        and hearing the music
        and people singing.
Her mother had said she shouldn't be
like those ladies upstairs across Bourbon
Street talking to the men.
They'd be cold with so few clothes on,
        she thought, if it weren't so warm.

She didn't understand that either,
        but her mother was as intense
as the hikers in her dream.
She'd like to go to the Northwest someday
        and hike with them.
They all seemed so free
        and it didn't matter to her that they
were tired and wet, and old.
She thought, though, she liked the downhill
        parts better
as she woke into the grey morning
        of her day.
They worked awfully hard to get uphill.
Maybe she'd find out who they were someday.

A Little Bumpy

"It's getting a little bumpy up here," he said.
    "You all better buckle up."
I see the parched desert below,
    sand and sagebrush
burned like extra crispy hash browns,
    small craters like moon dots
and the mesquite
    staring skull-like
at the scorching sun behind the plane.

I glimpse in the distance
    the twinkling dots of the rainbow
cascading down the 57th story
    of Mandalay Bay.
Tourists on the Pirates of the Caribbean
    sail round
the artificial Treasure Island
    fed with water
jack-hammered from the Colorado River.

Hotel after hotel,
MGM Grand, New York, New York, and Caesar's Palace,
    line the boulevards
offering privileged pleasure seekers
    the choice to bet
their life savings
    on the whimsical drop of a little white ball
into their slot on the spinning wheel.
This is no mirage.
They stare at the drop of a three of clubs,
    or the pull of the slot handle
as sweat trickles down
    into Hawaiian shirts
        and polyester sundresses.

They relax, cooled under the continuous hum
        of the air conditioners,
living the American Dream.

We cruise down through the clouds
        into the metropolis
        rising out of the desert
        living that same Dream.
A small voice seems to whisper,
        "Apres nous, c'est le deluge."*
We drop into the heat haze.

* *Attributed to Louis XV.*

Blowing In Rome

The wind blew
down the Santa Fe hills
through my hair
like those Gypsy
girls in Rome
that blew out of
the crowd
in the Piazza Navona
to lift my passport,
my money,
my wallet,
most of all, my self-respect.
Vulture-like,
they were after
my money
and took my vulnerability
as an afterthought.

The Aquifer In Magic Valley

I ride my bike early in the morning
        to miss the afternoon heat
and the loss of fluids
that would pour out my sweat glands.
The brilliant orange ball hangs
        just below the horizon
off to the east.
Red sky frames the light like a moving
        sun of Japan.
Sprinklers roll quietly through
        fields of wheat and alfalfa
doling out the precious water.

A diesel truck belching its fumes
        slides by my bike.
The bottle of pure spring water rests
        in my backpack
to be rationed judiciously.

I coast by the thousand springs
        in the Magic Valley.
Once, not long ago, water
        cascaded down the rock walls
of the northern face of the Snake River.
Today they are stone dry.

A lizard suns itself
        on a slice of rock
as the desert snake
glides silently through
the sagebrush
to the prairie dog's door.

Algae float below the water's surface
        clogging the river.
Herons that hovered in days past
        waiting just above
for a second helping of steelhead
have fled like
the dinosaurs that produced
        our diminishing oil reserves.

Seneca Consolidated assures us the water
        was needed for the aquifer
below ground,
so shouldn't be wasted
        cascading the rocks of the canyon.
They say the aquifer
will provide all the water
needed to grow our food
and maintain our lifestyle.
Forever.

I ride on in the growing heat.
The orange ball of the morning
        is now a brilliant red circle
ravaging the coolness of the afternoon.
The blacktop striking my tires
        protects the aquifer below
from the blasts of the sun's furnace.

I see a ground squirrel
        scurrying across the sandy ground
to his den opening behind the cactus.
Down he races,
        thirsty for water,
        running for his life.

Dazedly he slips into his familiar slot
        far underground,
            now bone dry
and damaged beyond recall.
There is no water today in the
        aquifer.

Fifth Grade At St. Aloysius

Catholic grade school circa 1955
after "Two-Room Schoolhouse"
by Nance Van Winckel

I know Sister Miriam can tell
when I haven't done my homework.
How she can see beyond her

starched white head brace
is a continual mystery to us all.
But we know she can.

Gazing today at the rippling pond,
silver rain dripping on grey ducks,
I think of that day I unknowingly

stepped over the invisible line.
Sister knew I had.
The class looked down at their desks.

She pointed to the blackboard.
She drew a small circle in the center,
two inches in diameter.

Her ruler rose slowly,
pointing finally at my nose.
"There," she said.

"Your nose," she said.
"Inside the circle
against the chalk board.

Now," she said.
"Stay," she said, "until you
remember not to do that again."

Today I sit remembering
how I got my nose right
inside that small white circle.

I didn't ever do that again
because my nose never went
back in the circle on the board.

I've been trying this whole
time to remember exactly
what it was I did.

The Bear Is Power

After "The Crow is Mischief"
by Laura Jensen

The bear is power.
He is the lord of the forest
as the snake is of the desert.

He shadows you
as you hike the dusty trail.
He forces you
to hang your food bag
high in a tree at night.

One time I saw a mother bear
with her cub
bolt out of the huckleberry bushes.
They ran right past us,
across the trail, not ten feet ahead.
I thought they were coming for us.

Instead they scrambled up
the nearest trees,
mother and son.

My heart pounded in my chest.
We clapped our hands "confidently,"
as the guide books advise.
Maybe they heard us.
Maybe God was with us.
Maybe they thought we knew
what we were doing.

We strode down the trail whistling.
Why they hung
onto their tree trunks
watching us go,
I'll never know.

The Promise Of The Trail

Dancing Moon Press
2013
Newport, Oregon

Introduction

The genesis of this book occurred during a reading by Paul Merchant at the Milwaukie Poetry Series in June 2010. Among Paul's many talents is that he is a translator of the books of Greek poet, Yannis Ritsos. One of the books I bought that evening was a copy of Ritsos's book, *Monochords.*

That book was published in 1967 while Ritsos was under house arrest. *Monochords* is a book of one-line poems, which do three things: 1) be a poem in itself; 2) be the start of a longer poem; and 3) reflect something of importance to the poet.

I decided to try a few poems in this style. After writing a set of 20, I decided to write another 20. That grew to 100, and then 180. And then 365. This book is the result. My interest was different from that of Ritsos, who had written long poems prior to *Monochords*. My interest was to master the form and say something of interest to the reader. Hopefully, *The Promise of the Trail Ahead* fulfills a bit of that.

The Promise Of The Trail Ahead: 1-20

After Monocords
by Yannis Ritsos

1. The promise of the trail ahead, inviting.

2. My mother left so much, some of it things to do.

3. The house sits on upright land.

4. The walking stick attacks all on its own.

5. Mice in my backpack, without paying rent.

6. At dawn, remember the promises.

7. Shamrock in sunlight; you are Irish.

8. Yellow bird warbles in the bath water.

9. Help with the world, it's too easy.

10. Two black crows swoop into the yard.

11. The pastor threw a monkey wrench today.

12. The white dog barks incessantly, sometimes to a purpose.

13. The parade draws down summer rain.

14. Love is as bottomless as the nearby well.

15. Black oil gushes on the gulf floor, still.

16. As I slept, the river rose twenty feet last night.

17. He has that vacant look today.

18. The monastery beckons to the next state.

19. Squirrels snatch their food on the deck railing, cat twitching along.

20. The church is the church, don't you know.

The Promise Of The Trail Ahead: 21-40

21. Samuel Johnson mesmerized in an English pub.

22. Coffee is a staple food, isn't it?

23. The news on the daily broadcast, rolling like an ocean wave, was rarely good.

24. Sugar constitutes the only sweetener we need, he thought.

25. A heart of gold arrives after a diligent search.

26. Red eyes in the night, searching.

27. The trail traipses uphill, then down.

28. We have the gifts we need, it was advertised.

29. A coyote prances into our campground.

30. Sometimes grief is too precious to be explored.

31. His rationale has been exposed.

32. Money is abundant, they say.

33. Two bears lounged within ten feet, eating huckleberries.

34. Facing St. Paul sometimes requires sunglasses.

35. America, they want to reward the rich, corrupt though they may be.

36. After ten years of waiting, the killer was caught today.

37. Develop a crush, wine tours galore.

38. You are very fast, my granddaughter!

39. Garbage goes out; collectibles come in.

40. The miners remained trapped 2200 feet below ground, surviving for four months.

The Promise Of The Trail Ahead: 41-50

41. Despair acknowledged, a step toward solution.

42. Sex is the softener of life.

43. I'm ready to clean the basement, it's so scary.

44. I bike for exercise, my hip not up to running. The doctor says he can fix it.

45. Having a plan feels better.

46. The waves rise and fall, in and out, continuously.

47. A daypack needs to be held with thumbs.

48. Faith, renewed regularly, is a precious gift.

49. Help comes creeping along, like a silver leaf slowly shifting.

50. The empty tomb confronts us.

New Poems
I

Listening For Epiphany

In Luke's version
camels loped
across sandy dunes
carrying their riders
to a manger just

southeast of Jerusalem.
The star shining
in the heavens
showed the way
to these men, called Magi.

Today we drive
rain-soaked streets in
Clackamas, Oregon,
searching for that same
promise in a manger.

Our guiding light
may be entirely
different from that
star in the sky.
If you are paying attention.

Poetry

Poetry is a supremely suitable lover.
She rides contentedly in the car for miles.

She stands patiently, contemplating the bayou,
eucalyptus reaching to the stagnant water.

She's a friend as the serpent slips out from the
mildew by the lilacs and slides up the bank.

When I'm alone at night with a blaze in the fireplace,
listening to the crickets, she stays up with me.

She laughs when I see the yellow sign with an
alligator image on it that reads, "No swimming!"

I can take her to a cocktail party as a sage
and not worry about being embarrassed.

When people ignore her benefits,
she just hangs around without being offended.

My First Connection With Poetry

The cards lay face-up
on the square green folding table
usually reserved for bridge;
the game today was Authors:
Dickens, Austen, Twain,
Tolstoy, Chekhov,
Longfellow.

Mother occupied herself
in the kitchen, selecting the correct
ingredients for the dinner meatloaf,
split pea soup simmering
on the stove, potatoes baking in tin foil
in the oven.

It was too late to change
my salt-and-pepper school
cords for evening jeans,
too early for TV,
too near dinner for a walk.
Who was Longfellow? I wondered,
as I pulled my mother's poetry book
from the bookcase.

Leafing through the book, I came upon
"The Song of Hiawatha,"
"Evangeline,"
finally "Paul Revere's Ride."

I wish I could say I fell in love
with Longfellow that day,
or even in fellowship with poetry.
We did finish our game of Authors

and I even learned
who Tennyson was as well.

Years later, we happened upon
a traffic jam near Cascade Locks,
Oregon, on I-84.
We were stopped.
As I stepped out of the Sentra,
the sun baked us to the
smarmy blacktop;
cars ahead were
backed up out of sight.

I looked in the back seat,
pulled out my *Collected Works
of Henry Wadsworth Longfellow*
in a collector's Modern Library edition
with the original dust jacket,
and read some "Evangeline."

Important things stick with you.

Start Of Another Beautiful Day

In the early morning light,
sun not yet risen,
I watch the neighborhood squirrels
scurry across the deck rail
rushing to the birdseed there,
aware always of the white miniature Samoyed
blocked by the sliding deck door.

I see two coal-black crows land beneath
the yellow Queen Anne rose bushes
in the garden, celery-like mist lying on the grass
newly cut last night, just before darkness
dropped like the curtain at a high
school production of *Oliver Twist*.

I watch our black cat, Tony, picking his way
through that grass, imagining he's
stalking a passing bluebird, his presence
telegraphed to any local thrushes that happen
to be awake. No bird is going to fly by a cat in plain
sight and let him grab her for breakfast.

Farther away, I see mist floating
on the Willamette River,
fishermen slipping their tackle boxes
into aluminum boats with a professional
silence designed to keep fish in their watery beds
until a tantalizing worm on a hook wakens
them from their nightly slumbers.

Janus View

I sit today on hard wooden planks
in the St. John the Baptist Catholic
School gym: blue banners on the wall,
Girl Scout cookies for sale in the entry,

my granddaughter, Emma, nine years old,
playing her first basketball game. Fourteen
fourth-grade girls in blue jerseys, she is #22,
in blue shorts, long and baggy as they wear

now, not the short pants I wore when
I played sixty years ago. A CYO prayer
about God, sportsmanship, and competing
ripples through the crowd just before tip-off.

Three other teams are in this jamboree,
two games next week, the next one four
days away. The thrill of youth, new
endeavors, causes palpable excitement.

I have to leave after her first game
for a rosary, then a funeral at 11 AM
at St. Agatha's Catholic Church: my
friend's wife, Pat, dead from cancer,

she Catholic, he not, evidencing a lifelong
accommodation. She died after struggling
with a long illness; not a total surprise.
I watch this Janus-like, new life before

my eyes in the gym, celebrating old life
in an hour, the passing of a time.
Janus lived this every moment, only
today it's more noticeable, the passage

dramatized like bookends on our regular
events of the day, as if headlines blazoned
in days past on the old *International Herald
Tribune*, today on the Comcast home page.

My High School English Teacher

He would sweep into the classroom
like a bustle of wind,
sometimes dragging leaves and twigs
along with his books and homework
to return to us.

Often he was on time, always in the ballpark.
He would pass those papers back
in some unconventional way, sometimes
alphabetically, sometimes in rows, sometimes by grades—
always a mystery how we would get them back,
with comments, sometimes even to the point,
often understandable.

I don't remember what books
this slender Italian priest,
Father Anthony Juliano, had us read
or what poems he watched us recite
through his black horn-rimmed glasses,
what mysteries of *Moby Dick* he revealed
while glancing sometimes at his quietly
ostentatious black Rolex watch.

But I do remember
his love of musicals,
his staging of our annual high school plays,
his excitement and ours over
what they would be,
who would be in shows like:
Finian's Rainbow, Brigadoon,
My Fair Lady.

I do remember him casting
me in the play, *Allegro*,
which I'd never heard of,
as the old steel magnate Chairman of the Board
who wanted the mill to run better,
cheaper, and more often.

I do remember I had grey hair and had to be
in makeup for a half an hour each night.

I do remember I smoked a cigar
as part of my character when I
delivered crunching news.

I do remember one night, that I, on my own initiative,
lit my cigar too early,
was standing backstage ready to go on.
I smelled very "in character."

I do remember him coming up to me,
growling: "Put out that damned cigar."
With that direction, I had to go on in one minute.
I don't remember flubbing my lines
or getting booed off the stage.
I must have done all right.

And I do remember with fondness
my high school English teacher,
the Italian priest Father Juliano.

Birthday

My frosting went on smoothly for a change,
lemon this time, for a person with a sweet tooth,

someone, I understand, who doesn't really like
cakes but wants one with candles for tradition's sake.

I heard that yesterday when he made his order.
I was sitting in my baker's bin waiting for something

to happen and in he comes, proclaiming "a cake
to go by end of the week, white with lemon

frosting, Happy Birthday on it." Of course he
would say that, everybody does, but it fits the

occasion. He looked like a pleasant man,
glasses, a little older than I thought he would be

from what the baker confided after taking his call.
We'll have to see, for I heard he's having a party

tomorrow. I know I'm going to love being part
of that; it's so special being the center of attention

when bringing joy to folks as they celebrate their
entry into the world of humans. In my case, I've

discovered it's a little like that Bill Murray movie
where he kept coming back till he got it right.

Ground Hog Day, I think it was. Tomorrow
will be all too fleeting at the party unfortunately,

but I've found that, being a cake, I'll rise
again soon, this time maybe as chocolate.

To My 24-Year-Old Self

"Hello, my friend,"
waiting in line
at the Draft Board Office,
West Los Angeles, California,
August 24, 1967,
ready to take your physical exam.
You're good looking
but unsure of yourself,
I can see.
You passed me on the street,
not giving me
even a glance,
so tied up in your
struggles with the war,
the future,
the right
place to live, in finding
the right key to
unlock the door
which says,
"Doing the right thing."
I see you're trying
and if you could hear
me, I'd say you have
a guardian angel
on your right shoulder,
right now.
He'll stay with you.
Listen to him,
I'd say softly,
"He'll protect
you."

Fortune Cookie

"You will be unlucky in love,"
the sweet fortune cookie fortune
proclaimed, like a thirty-six point
headline in the *New York Times*.

Was this a portent to take seriously?

It might predict future failings, possibly
a quivering morass of quicksand ahead,
my hope for love fading like yesterday's
coffee washed down the kitchen drain.

Or it might show a mountain to be scaled,
like an Eighth Labor of Hercules

erected by the gods to prove worthiness
to earn the love of my dreams.
I ate the cookie
while pondering the prediction,
suddenly aware that it's in the future.

I don't know the outcome yet
of the fortune cookie's sweet fortune.

Things That Happened Since I Heard

After Linda Kasischke
"Things That Have Changed Since You Died"

The morning after I heard, I sat at my computer
and heard a bump, bump, bump
at the basement window.
Made reservations at the Quality Inn
     in Placentia, California,
one town away from Orange and
your funeral.

Finished the book you recommended
at our last conversation, *Nearing Home,*
     by Billy Graham, still alive,
about preparing to die.

Talked to my friend Carolyn about how she is,
and left my to-do list till the evening.

Visited Dwayne in the hospital
and found our mutual friend Lee
     in the next room.
"What's the plan," I asked and
Lee said, "There is no plan—
I'm going home to die."

Called four rental agencies in Los Angeles
to book the car we wanted.

Read yesterday that rock star Prince died and
wondered if you would know
who he was.

Went to the basement window to discover
          the bumping was a blue jay
trying to fly in the window, and knew you
would have been interested in that.

Went to Mass,
my wife, Jane, has kept getting better,
gave a poetry reading,
wrote a lot of e-mails,
talked to people that I wouldn't have
          six months ago
because I missed talking to you.
I could go on

and on and I know you'd say,
quoting Billy Graham,
"Will see you someday."

I'm Not Ready To Be Grateful

After Glen's death

They say you should be grateful for everything.
It's something I've been working on,
learning to appreciate my toothache
and the Dupuytrens Contracture,
my car stopping in traffic on the way
to the poetry reading one night,

our friend not showing up
when he said he would. This frosty
morning, though, I knelt in the hospital room
holding your body as it grew colder,
thinking, I'm grateful for this time now,
given that this happened.

That's always how it is: "given
that this has happened." The McKenzie
River flows along outside the hospital,
a yellow finch cheeps on the nearby limb,
a family sleeps in the waiting room.
How can I ever be grateful for

this death, so fast, so unpredicted?
I think of how God's ways are
not our ways, maybe, but it mystifies me
as gratitude continues to elude.
Acceptance is different from gratitude.
That's all I can muster today.

Accounting

After The Years
by Michael Hoffman

I gave an account of myself
even though I didn't have to.

I might have avoided it altogether
if he hadn't seemed interested.

He had no questions, no response.
Then he talked about himself.

First Camp

After "Homesick"
by Jane Kenyon

Here at Boy Scout Camp at Lost Lake near
      white-capped Mt. Hood,
there's no refrigerator in the next room
      like at home
to get a glass of Hood River apple juice.

Mosquitoes buzz around my head,
      swarming to procreate.
Yesterday I even swallowed one,
      gagging as I felt its legs
tickle my throat.

Last night ants crept into my spaghetti
      saved from dinner
for a midnight snack in our ridiculously
      small pup tent.
They had brought half the nest, it seemed.

I remember sitting in front of the knot board
      challenged to tie
five knots in one minute to get the merit badge
      they said I wanted.
Our scoutmaster, Mr. Naylor, demonstrated

tying the knots, no mosquitoes around his head.
      Then one by one,
the boys succeeded getting their badges.
      I remember a mosquito
landing on my thumb as I tied the first knot.

Later I would tell my parents I loved seeing
      Mt. Hood, rowed
across the lake in under four minutes, and even
      learned the difference
between a square knot and a granny.

My Cell Phone

The silver rectangle lies pulsating
on the desk near my right hand.

An arcane marking at the bottom
resembles an upside down W

that's not exactly an M.
Back plastic buttons on the side,

soft rubber on the corners,
a globe with longitudinal lines

implies a portal to the world.
Its blue-black front resembles

a mirror that reveals
in its misty depths that I need a shave.

The eyes behind the mirror whisper:

I can do a lot for you.
Open me up.
Turn me on.
Use me.
I can show you vistas
you never could have imagined.

I've heard all that before,
my small voice replies.

The Delight Song Of Tom Hogan

After The Delight Song of Tsoai-talee
by N. Scott Momaday

I am an oak tree, branches providing shade.
I am Puget Sound lapping at the ferry docks.
I am the black crow standing in the bike lane.
I am a salmon cascading to sea.
I am the brown bear retreating from the summer campground.
I am the Pacific Crest Trail running
        from Mexico to Canada.
I am an organic banana.
I am orange carrots on the dish tray.
I am twilight at Jasper National Park
        at 10:30 at night.
I am Mercury hurrying across the night sky.
You see, I am alive, I am alive.
I am earthworm tunnels under the grass.
I am 10,000 crickets chirping at dusk.
I am the song of robins singing in the morning.
I am lilacs swaying in the spring breeze.
I am the smell of darkness in dead of night.
I am in good relation to my body.
I am in good relation to the earth.
I am in good relation to God.
I am in good relation to all that I hold dear.
I am in good relation to my dear ones.
You see, I am alive, I am alive.

Lists

After Lists
by Linda Pastan

I made a list of things I need
to forget; that list turned out to be
just as long as the list of things
to remember. Even on the list
of things to accomplish, I have
to remember to move those
items from yesterday's list
to the new one till they're done.

On my list to remember was
that Jefferson thought slavery
would die out by 1808, twenty
years after the Constitution
was ratified. He was wrong.
I need to remember that.
Perhaps he made a list of his own:
buy salt, write Adams, free slaves.

Time With Maria

For Maria Aikin

I was dumbfounded. It was a call out of
the blue—the Gladstone Police Chief with
"Not so good news," Maria died yesterday.

It can't be true, I thought. Never in a
million years would I have guessed that
was the message he wanted to give me.

Maria was so vibrant, so alive, so "here."
I was incredibly grateful for the time she and
I spent that August Thursday when she came

to visit me after surgery. We had tried to do it
several weeks earlier, but had to change plans.
Then her workload exploded. I was partly okay

with that because I didn't always like to talk about
my health. I was a lot better, but not totally well
when I wanted to be well. She came at 3—

I thought she'd stay an hour. We covered
the ground, as you could do with Maria.
What about Wendy? How was the Chief?

Barbara lived a long way away and we didn't
see her as often as we liked. We went over what
was happening in Gladstone: some new, some

"same old-same old." Four o'clock came and I had
something else that needed doing. Then
the little voice said, "This is more important,
you don't need to rush off. You may not get this

chance again." So we talked till 5. The sun
was out, the day was beautiful. We sat
on the patio in the shade and, as they used

to say, visited. This time we really covered
the ground. To this day, no matter how hard
I've tried, I still don't remember what seemed

so important to rush off. The small voice
came through when I slowed down,
listening, allowed to spend my time with Maria.

For Joe

At the retirement of Ledding Librarian, Joe Sandfort

"Don't worry about it," he said. "I'll take care
of it." And I knew he would, with dispatch.

Geese stopped cars on Harrison Street as we
talked, nutria climbed out of the nearby Pond,

lights of the library gleamed in the early dusk.
I know he's a Giants fan, I thought. I wonder if he

remembers Regal Select beer in a bottle for a buck
at Candlestick Park. In those days they let you have

the bottle. Joe slides into retirement with the grace
of a Matt Cain* curve hitting the strike zone.

In the time I've written this, he's taken care of it.
Just one of the many qualities we cherish.

* A pitcher for the San Francisco Giants.

Silver Window

I am a silver window in my Milwaukie home,
helping my humans see the larger world.
I gaze out all day at drivers rushing about;
yellow school buses push one way in the morning,
the opposite in the afternoon.

Sometimes it rains crocus-hard;
other days the sunlight lets me
see even our neighbor's cat looking
both ways before crossing the street.

Today a warm-blooded Indian
just out of jail mows the grass.
I see the postman delivering our mail.
One day last week seven ambulances
streamed by with sirens blaring.
A man died last Tuesday just outside
on his way to the hospital.

Today I see blue jays in the oak trees.
A white dog on a leash struggles forward.
A woman picks up her poodle's leavings.
I watch and bleed and laugh with them.

Asparagus Today

Silky green stalks stared languidly at me
from the serving dish that family dinner,
passed from uncle to cousin just between
the candied yams and the hot brown gravy.
Picked new from the fields yesterday,
so fresh, they said, it will leave its tiny
footprints on your tongue.
It was my turn next.
I struggled not to wince as the platter
eased into my sweating hands.

That day in my childhood the asparagus
had sand in it,
grating on my frightened tongue.
Mercifully, my Aunt Kathryn sided
with me and said that the sand was no figment
from the basement of my frivolous imagination.
They thought I just didn't want to eat it.
My mother told the story over and over.
It grew into family lore.

Will it be the same this Easter family dinner?
Tonight my granddaughter
hands me the porcelain serving plate.
Green asparagus stalks stare at me
once again, sliding onto my plate.
My teeth bite into soft green tissue.
Juice sweeter than honey vines
slides along the soft stem.
Tonight it is different.

Yet To Live

In response to Osip Mandelstam's poem,
"Yet to Die"

Yet to live. Together at last.
For all your joys are with you now
together in morning sun's grandeur
or the first inkling of blue-black night.

Live peaceful and contented
in the powerful lap of unguarded prayer
to help lift those submerged in grinding poverty
or suffering the hook of the Guardia worm.

I want to live loving those I meet on life's path,
listening to the voices clamoring for shelter,
for peace, rich in our love to help those in need.
I ride that road with you, my brothers and sisters.

A Step Up In Purgatory

Heavy fog shrouds the river.
Clouds hold the sun hostage,
        allowing minimal warmth
to seep through their billows.
Morning dew coats cars
        resting in the driveway.
My friend calls.
I offer thanks.
Our dog gets a run.
I say a prayer for my friend's wife who has cancer.
I offer to split a donation for a Fred Meyer project.
The fog starts to lift.
The day progresses, offering
unlimited opportunities —
tiny steps up the seven-story mountain
        of Purgatory.

More To Do

I

I drove the streets of downtown Portland
      this Good Friday morning,
saw men walking with no place to go,
      a dwarf on crutches,
people sprawled on blankets on the sidewalk,
a young woman with a baby and a sign,
      a person with a face
disfigured from birth or a splash of
      hydrochloric acid,
      I wasn't sure.

I watched a homeless man walking
      in the crosswalk
      by the Blanchet House;
he slowed enough to make sure I
      stopped for him.
Later, I saw him at the Union Gospel
      Mission,
slouched in line, smoking a cigarette,
      whiling away his time.

I didn't plan to become open today
      to this level of suffering.

II

Later in the day
I made the Walk of the Cross,
      noon to three o'clock,
      ten Stations in all,
each one a topic proclaiming our needs,
      our failures, our hopes.

Between Station Five, on prostitution,
        and Station Six, on human
trafficking, we passed
        a Gentleman's Club,
one of six in a seven-block area,
        its doors open,
dark inside, a tunnel.
        I looked to see what allure
there could be
        at 2:30 in the afternoon,
no nude dancers
performing at this hour.
I wanted to shout, "Come out
        before it's too late."

At the last Station on immigration,
I heard a Hispanic mother
        telling us she is being forced
to leave the country, to leave her three sons
        here in the county
while she moves out of the country
so she can move back into the country,
        with a probable green card.
Her tears flowed and a woman moved
        to hug her.

I wondered if this may have been the way
        Jesus walked
        that Good Friday,
his eyes saying,
"I know you've done a lot already,
        I know it's hard
            to do 'more.'
These ask you to."

New Poems
II

To Be At Cathlamet

A shot in the green Chevy.
Parked by the dark-greenish river
at Cathlamet, Washington.
A bullet in her brain
ended Rachel's life
in a microsecond.

I ask as I sit at the
memorial service
in a northeast Portland school
celebrating a life
lived like the kayaker she was.

Her boyfriend recounts that she saw
sixty-five doctors
in the past three months.
Her pain, on a good day,
was a ripe seven.

Her estranged father reads
a statement of his
anguish and attempts
over the years
to communicate,
the parent-child disharmony
too strong to bridge.

Her brother says he loved her,
and a kayaking colleague
tells about shooting a
Class Five rapid
that was a Class Six before someone rode it.

It's going to be my turn to speak
in a micro minute.
I'll say the best I can.
But if I had my choice
I'd be at Cathlamet
by the dark Columbia
with a chance to prevent
the gunshot coming up next.

The Sanctuary

After "The Sacred"
by Stephen Dunn

She asked if I had a sacred place
where I went for comfort, to be alone,

not someplace so far away I'd go only
once in a blue moon. And I said, "I was

just there," Sunday, May 22, 2016,
on the Horsetail Falls—Oneonta Gorge

Trail. Many times before, I'd driven up the
Columbia River to escape the crowd,

to be in nature, to hike, to get stress relief.
It's the first hike of the season, and the last

in the fall, in November, rain or shine. Today,
I can almost glimpse the bridge below

taking us across the ravine. Birds chirp
around me, air hangs lightly, Oneonta

Creek flows along through the gorge like
a Mozart sonata and endorphins slip

into my blood stream. I came here last year,
the year before, twenty-five years ago;

this day I'm here again with you. My worries
are partying together in the city—I'll keep coming,

keep returning,
my love, into your beautiful green boudoir.

Around The Corner

This morning, just past sunrise
        I dreamt of the gray-green water
of the Perdernales rushing over rocks
        resting in the river bed.
Sagebrush rolled up the brown hills
        of the country west of Austin,
wild bluebonnets and
        Indian paintbrush
sprouting between occasional cacti.

I glided along the river
        in the crisp morning,
stepping by a diamondback
        rattlesnake sunning
itself on brown baked rocks,
        waiting
for a Texas pica to emerge
        from its dark hole
into the brilliant morning.

The river waves lapped
        on the shore
like the currents I
        imagine carried
the curved ships of heroic Odysseus
        past the Siren's
beckoning song, past the banks
        of the River Styx,
past Calypso's Island to Ithaca.

I pulled at the sheets hot
        with night sweat
and ruffled the flowered pillow,
        straining my shaded

eyes to glimpse around the bend
		as the river ahead
curved sharply to the right.
		The turn was upon me before
I could ever see around the corner.

East To Orlando

Our 737 jet reclined on the tarmac forty-five
minutes, seventeen other planes ahead of us,

before lifting off into the blue sky.
A sudden thunderstorm over Houston

forced us to land in Austin
before we ran out of gas circling.

Now another storm brewing to the east
forces our flight inland from the Gulf

past New Orleans, past Biloxi, past
Mobile, on to Orlando. Downtown

Houston sprawls twenty-two miles
away like Oz rising out of the clouds.

In the east, evening slowly drifts in
as we edge around the storm, water

everywhere below. "Not to worry,"
the pilot reassures us. "We'll be out

of the woods in just a few minutes."
Houston has so much water around it,

much more that I ever thought possible
for a city inland from the Gulf.

Rain beats down and we fly on.
I hope the convention is worth it.

Mt. Vernon Morning

John Marshall visiting President Washington

Mist drifts lazily off the Potomac
in the early March
dawn. The three-year-old chestnut

struts and paws ground hard
with frost while snorting
into the late winter chill.

He's itching to ride down home to
Richmond. I must say "no" again
and again, more forcefully,

if that's what is necessary to avoid this
supreme discomfort. There is the
plantation and my wife's people;

certainly my legal work on the
Virginia Circuit. He knows all this.
And still he persists.

Last night at dinner it was this again,
done so skillfully as to pressure
me but avoid embarrassment for the ladies.

Madison knows what he wants,
I'm sure, so then Mrs. Madison.
And Jefferson as well.

He said Jefferson was indispensable
too, and it was off to State.
He's been up before me, I see.

A sleepless night, he says.
We've been over this ground
a dozen times. Why would he

want me for Chief Justice?
It's a thankless, pointless position.
No, it's impossible, out of the question.

The Pulpit At The Seaman's Bethel

The pulpit in the Seaman's Bethel
looked like any ordinary one
except it had a ship's prow jutting
outward toward the congregation,
as it did in Melville's day. He sat
in the balcony, second row, to the right,
before shipping out for a year and a half
in the voyage that became Moby Dick.

The Seaman's Bethel is here today,
in the National Park in New Bedford,
Massachusetts. We watched transfixed,
imagining the words of Father Mapple
cascading over the outstretched prow.

"It wasn't that way then," said the National
Park Service guide. "The prow used to be
in back, always was, since the beginning of
Seaman's Bethel in the 1840s." But people
always asked where it was, as in the movie,
the prow clearly in front. John Huston
thought it much more cinematic that
Orson Welles deliver Father Mapple's
sermon over that prow—it seemed
to carry the pastor's words heavenward.

"We used to tell them," the guide says,
"that was just a movie." But the people
kept asking about the prow. So one
day, the Park Service decided
to move the prow to the front,
jutting from the pulpit,

just as we see it today,
just the way it was in the movie.
There have been no complaints since.

>Moby Dick *published by Herman Melville in 1851.*
The movie, Moby Dick, *was directed by John Huston,*
and released in 1956.

STAGECOACH

For John Wayne and John Ford

He wondered what it would be like to swing
the rifle the way he did.
He didn't know where that came from.
He was sure his friend, the Director,
that insufferable sphinx, wanted him to do something

but wouldn't tell him what that was.
He couldn't know in his wildest dreams
the impact it would have,
that the camera would sweep in,
recording the electricity of his entrance.

All his stardom was in the future.
He'd been laboring in the "B" pits
for eleven years waiting for something
to happen, that big chance,
not knowing when it would be.
Someday, he thought,
someday, if I'm paying attention.

Usually he had to do a scene
over and over
until the Director thought it was good.
This time the first take seemed right.
He trusted that one-eyed Irishman
to put it in the film.

Now we can see it anytime:
the swing that made a star.

Sunday In Washington, D.C.

Strolling Sunday in the Hirshhorn Gallery, we
drift toward the "Dream," the statue of Balzac,

staring off into the horizon like a meditating
Aquinas contemplating the Trinity. Reddish-brown

leaves swirl around its bronze base on this fall day.
The Washington Monument stands fully erect

down the Mall as tiny sparrows flit under
Balzac's muscular arms and Eastern swallows

land in the branches nearby. The Capitol looms
in the opposite direction, outlined against the haze

remaining from the morning mist. Can life come
together as symmetrically as this Mall? I reflected

on Balzac's great panorama of post-Napoleonic
society, *La Comedie Humaine*. Sometimes,

like an out-of-focus kaleidoscope, life's puzzle
comes into sharp view with a slight turn of the wheel.

We hear the distant faint rumble of the
Washington Metro far underground.

A Kiwi Voice

On a trip to New Zealand.

"Lost your voice,
have you, mate?" he cackled
through teeth yellowed by cigarette smoke.
He was wearing a brown cap over
hair threatening gray.

We were walking on a New Zealand street
in Taranga on the North Island
and it was true.
No poems were slipping out as
our group mangled tranquility,
sliding across country shires
on the wrong side of the road.

I'm like an 180-pound Kiwi, I thought,
who can't fly
and shyly displays
a nocturnal personality.

"No worries, mate," I tell him.
"It'll come back." Like
the swallows to Capistrano.
At least that's how I'm telling it.

Counterintuitive Move

"We've sold our house and are moving to Phoenix,"
he said, and I wondered why they would be doing that

when water is going to be the next giant problem
pushing people to move from Phoenix to Portland.

At least that's what we would be doing. Moving to
Phoenix in summer would be heading into a furnace.

But they have a different way of looking at life
and what they want to do. It seemed to be a huge

mistake, one that would be very hard to rectify,
but they are committed. Their house is sold

and they're going at the end of the month. A friend
gave me his verdict: "That's the way you learn."

Milwaukie City Hall

For the 75th Anniversary

It seemed a fairy tale in late 1936
when Milwaukie learned that the new
City Hall, long overdue, some said,
would be constructed: two stories, of deep
magenta brick fired in a local county kiln.

The Regional Director of the PWA* said it
was possible. Not only that, they wanted
to do it. FDR made this happen, as with
hundreds of other projects across the country
during this Depression, when workers laid brick a dollar
an hour, and one named Don left some of his soul
on the ceiling of the City Hall in what is now the Work
Session room. On some days when the light
is just right, you may be able to make it out.

For more than seven decades, City Hall has endured,
more than a diamond in the rough, lifting
the City up through the past, anchoring
it all the way to the present, like a pulsating
organism out of Carl Sandburg's "Chicago."

Today, maples flourish outside the City
Manager's window of a City Hall that lives
as a center for all who need its breath:
for Eldon, a farmer, coming for his land report,
Mr. Jeffers, the contractor, for his water permits,
planning committee folks projecting the future,
the judge arriving for his Traffic Court,
a just-married receptionist filing her nails
before fingering her computer, a reluctant
teenager slouching in to pay his littering ticket.

Engaged, constantly evolving,
avoiding the acedia befalling other cities,
Milwaukie City Hall at seventy-five
nurtures the City still, streamlining like a
Burlington Zephyr on track to the future.

*Until 1939, The Federal Emergency
Administration of Public Works
used the acronym PWA,
a New Deal program.*

At The Track Meet

Tents—blue, green and white—dot the LaSalle
High School track field and sidelines

sheltering kids waiting for their event. Roses
and trilliums bloom in the flower beds lying

next to the school windows. Sunlight
breaks through the clouds as a rainbow

rising after the storm. Fragrances of coffee
and popcorn waft from the snack bar, young

athletes lean against the stands stretching
their Achilles tendons. Kids dart back and forth

in anxious anticipation. My eleven-year-old
granddaughter, Emma, streaks from the starting

line, a sixth grader competing in her fourth track
meet, her torso long and limber, almost no body fat
as with all the great runners; sleek black leggings
and trunks to minimize wind resistance.

Sitting on my second-row bench in the bleachers,
my smile broadens as she whips along Lane Two

toward the finish line. Later, I hand her
five dollars for the snack bar, her mother

insisting, "You have to get one nutritious thing;
popcorn is fine." "Okay," she says, "Thanks,

Grandpa," with a hug that melts any frost that
might be hanging on from the pre-race warm-up.

Mother Bear And Her Cub

Who would have thought the 1950s Colortone Post Card
could be so evocative? The caption on the back says that
this is a "fascinating picture" where the "little cub" receives
his first lesson in "The art of entertaining visitors in Yellowstone
National Park." The two brown bears walked in single file
across the dusty open area between evergreen glades.
But what I saw was the great grizzly mauling Leonardo
diCaprio in *The Revenant,* and wondering how they ever
got that footage of the bear treating Leo like a rag doll.

What is it that invites us to read our own story onto
straightforward pictures? Why is it that old photos
seem more expressive? Why do I wonder if this little
cub, born in 1955, ended his life in a zoo, or was urban-
renewaled onto a reservation? How is it that the color
seemed truer than the actual digital pictures we
see today? I looked at the picture again and thought:
be happy you are in a poetry workshop, February 2018;
enjoy that you have a car to get you home; be appreciative
that you aren't being mauled by a grizzly bear, movie or not.

At The Marian Shrine In Orlando

"You only have to improve 2 percent," he said.
"Most people have a hard time
grasping that."
It was confession time at the Basilica.
I was in deep water a long way from home.
Ultraviolet rays beat down on the Sunkist oranges,
alligators lay in the swamp just beyond
the latest housing developments for retirees.
I hope they don't fall into the swamp.
You never, ever see anyone swimming
other than in a pool or in the ocean.
I wondered if those were sharks swimming
in the lagoons near Disney World.

I thought a change in my life
had to be a 180-degree switch.
Move your life around today.
I looked under the rock in my conscience,
like the one you find in the garden
or out in the desert
with a sprawling anthill under it.
It's really like turning an aircraft carrier
a few degrees at a time.

The priest was talking to me, I remember.
I see why he's here at the Shrine,
forgiving people from all over the world.
"Don't cover up your insecurity," he says.
"What you fear and resist will come true.
Open your heart and shift just a little."

"Thank you very much" I said,
and left.
Once I took his counsel I knew
I would feel wonderful.
I walked out the church door.
No alligators in the ponds,
no sharks across the street,
the bookstore selling rosaries,
the tourists coming in droves.
Now the hard work begins.

Cold Front In Downtown Eugene

We saw people sleeping outside this evening in tents
or under tarps beneath the freeway overpasses,

the temperature in downtown Eugene holding
at a frigid nine degrees, chilling to the bone to be outside

the car for five minutes, much worse living outside.
How can this be, I thought, in the richest country

on earth? Ice hung on the tent poles, and you said,
"It's a case of the haves and the have nots and

we're some of the haves." I thought about that and said,
"You can see it clearly on cruises: we are the passengers,

and the servers are from third-world countries."
I won't be going on any more cruises, I thought.

But does that help with those sleeping outside in tents
in downtown Eugene? We thought about that some more,

then got out of the car and gave a man on the corner
three dollars. We drove along for a bit, thought some more,

said some prayers, then went home. What else was there
to do that evening in the cold front in downtown Eugene?

Desert Corners

Yesterday I imagined walking into a desert
alive with cactus and scorpions
as the Disney World entrance appears
on Florida Highway 536
as if by magic.
Somewhere it's always a desert.

All my bright dreams remain
in the green lawns of the city
of my youth in the Pacific Northwest.
Haunting memories gather to move
the muddy sun to evening.

The desert's life is in corners and pockets,
its waste and space,
its wildness.
In the crevices are its
color and life.
Look closely at your desert.

Give into the loneliness of the mountains,
get up alone in the night to pray,
walk down Main Street
onto the rolling promenade
searching for
an oasis to rest overnight.

I dream of crystalline
grace emerging
in the day's light shining on palms trees
off in the distance
in the Magic Kingdom
as the old paddle wheeler
slides into the dock.

Oil On The Gulf

The twin-engine shrimp boat
slid into its berth in Biloxi harbor.
Prime Louisiana shrimp ready
for the New Orleans market
rested on ice in the hold.

The ship aborted the day's run
three hundred yards from the
yellow booms in the choppy water
preventing the black oil gushing from
the Gulf floor wound from
spilling onto the shrimp beds.

Rain loomed over the shrimpers
like vultures circling a thirsty horse
alone in the mid-day desert.
Black oil slipped along with the current
coating everything in its path.

Deep resignation looms in the
captain's tired eyes
as he imagines the oil drift
swirling over the coast.

No more seafood.
No more shrimp.
No more swimming.
But tomorrow it could be different, he thought.
Maybe the booms will hold.

At The Veterans' Workshop

An American flag sits propped in a plastic cup as I
squirm to write about the soldier I talked with
last week, tattoos swirling on his calves,
struggling to stay intact through the shrapnel
of his daily life, metal shards pulsing
constantly from his childhood war zone.

He wants to pull his 9mm as he did in Iraq
when he could shoot his enemies hiding
behind the next hill, or haul out
the Browning grenade launcher he used to survive
the firefight in Zone K-75. Now, defenses
other than automatic weapons are required:
a comment here,
some listening there,
his Jack Daniel's bottle
left on the shelf,
the same shrewdness that allowed
Wyatt Earp to walk away from the
OK Corral to a life in Hollywood.
This one can do it.

Cold Coffee In Iraq

The cold coffee didn't do it for me
this morning hunched between these dusty
rocks waiting for something to happen,
temperature pushing 110 degrees.

I can never decide what's worse,
the waiting or the action,
as my thoughts turn to
Pierre at the Battle of Borodino.*

Those who died that day were involved
in a great defense of Mother Russia,
weren't they,
at least those on the right side?

Here I am sitting in Outpost 501,
47 miles north of Baghdad.
A Sunni warrior looking
down his AK47 right now
could squeeze the trigger,
I'm gone, no chance
to say goodbye, no way to know
anything about him, no moment
to wonder where I'm headed.

The cold coffee seems so far away now,
sitting between my dusty rocks,
going from moment to moment.
Only the next moment is real.

A fly saunters past my sunglasses.
The moment passes,
no action flowing like an ocean
wave over us,
no bullet this time,
just the buzzing of the flies.

* Pierre Bezukhov
Battle of Borodino, Sept. 7, 1812,
from War and Peace, *by Leo Tolstoy*

Evening At Bridal Veil

This evening was supposed to be the holiday
gathering, our Earth School Advisory Board

with Sister Suzanne and Sister Miriam, but
weather intervened; the promise of an ice

storm slid in. They cancelled the meeting
but we didn't get the message, showed up anyway.

What an honor, it turned out, to say Vespers
with the house of Sisters, then have dinner with them.

We enjoyed talking about the school, our pasts, Connecticut,
God, the Midwest, and the New England Patriots.

What a privilege! All from missing the message, making
an effort anyway, and discovering a special evening.

On The Pacific Crest Trail

With great anticipation he plunged his foot
into Crag Lake twelve miles north of Mt. Rainier.

He'd seen Karen, one of his partners on the pack,
do it just ten minutes earlier. He even met her

returning in full rapture from her foot-soaking time.
She had the foresight to bring a wash cloth;

he was trusting to the sun, the grass, and his shirt
to dry his feet. A gentle westerly breeze fanned

the water; the sun still lingered two hours above
the horizon, the mosquitoes blessedly absent.

No storm clouds hovered as they had the night before,
no rolling thunder announced a downpour.

A convenient log on which to bask lay on the
lake bank. With every expectation of delight,

in went the right foot—three inches into mud! Over
his foot it flowed, oozing between the toes, covering

them in mountain blackness. In went the left foot—
mud again. Where was the pristine lake water he

was expecting? That's continually how it is:
a charming surface hides hidden obstacles. Like Dante

struggling to describe the ascent of the *Purgatorio*,
he felt tongue-tied to relate this sudden, unexpected

irony. Then an auspicious thought bubbled forth!
The group planned to share something exciting

from the day at the evening campfire. Now he had
an occurrence different from what he planned. Later

it might even become a poem. As if on cue, he heard
his companion, Dennis, exclaim, "I think I'll have

a plum," and wondered if, like William Carlos Williams,
Dennis was going to confess to having eaten them all.

Instructions On How To Distinguish A Flower From A Frog

After Julio Cortázar

Begin by getting your garden chair from the garage.
Don't worry about the mosquito netting today. Pick
a time of day with moderate sunshine. Situate
yourself by the pond behind the rhododendrons.
Use the hose to bring in water if necessary.
Continue by observing that the flowers, roses,
geraniums, it doesn't matter, don't move. They are
stationary. They invite admiration. They all have
individual characteristics so you can tell them apart.

Next, observe that you may not see a frog.
You may never have seen a frog. Don't blame
yourself for this lapse—it may be inevitable.
Understand that the frogs, unlike flowers, like
to move around. They aren't stationary. They
don't ask to be admired. They all look alike,
although some are bigger. And they croak. They
don't just sit there and bask in the light. Surrender
to ecstasy if you have the great fortune to see a frog.

Milwaukie Train

My ears hear the Western Pacific whistle
its way across the arched trestle over
Kellogg Lake into downtown Milwaukie,

past the century-old high school,
past the library's Pond House
poets inside sweating to create,

past the swimming geese,
past ducks walking the road,
into my waiting heart.

New Poems
III

Giving Thanks

> *We should strive to be grateful*
> *for everything coming from God.*
> *Buddha*

The long-tailed squirrel frisks along the deck rail,
a deep-blue Stellar Jay drinks from the birdbath,
two coal-black crows perch on the weeping willow,
and the tiny spider slips off the plant limb.
    Thank you very much.

A braided rug covers the upstairs floor,
hot, sugared coffee steams in the cup,
my crimson writing pen has ink to spare
and the space heater fans heat into the chill.
    Thank you very much.

My friend in Maine didn't call this week,
the fire marshal doesn't answer his e-mails,
preparedness is a just a goal to many
and tasks pile up everywhere.
    Thank you very much.

Black oil lies under the carburetor,
our dog poops on the just-cleaned carpet,
both cats spit up last night's dinner
and fruit flies hover over the garbage.
    Thank you very much.

No one answers a request for more information,
my daughter and granddaughter go to California,
our oldest friend departs to his sister's,
work increases even as we finish each task.
    Thank you very much.

The Trail Blazers win their game at the last second,
I read a new vaccine will diminish Alzheimer's,
terrorists attack tourist hotels in India,
and Britney Spears is succeeding in her comeback.
      Thank you very much.

A bonus check arrives unexpectedly in the mail,
people volunteer for service at the Red Cross,
I ask for help with the day's tasks
and my hip hurts a little more today.
      Thank you very much.

Near Blue Box Pass

Even now, the feel of the wheel in my hands comes back,
After the failure of the tires to grip the icy black road,
The smell of helplessness as the car slides sideways
Near Blue Box Pass on Mt. Hood on a clear, starry night.

Earlier that day, returning from winter skiing at Mt Bachelor,
Away late, driving tired, when the black ice materialized
On a curve, letting me glimpse the drop-off on the right as
The Rover slid around, slamming into the snow bank on the left.

I remember sitting in the driver's seat turning the engine key
On and off, trying to start an obviously wrecked car,
Sweat glistening down my arms and the whiffs of gasoline
Kicked up by the car's sudden impact floating on the breeze.

Love lives so near as I write this, remembering my fear,
And the delicious gratitude for the life I hold so dear.

ON USING WORDS

For St. Francis of Assisi

In her sermon Sunday morning at
Saint Francis Catholic Church,
our pastor spoke as eloquently as
she ever has on these political topics:

she said Jesus came to help the poor,
He did it for justice and love but
the social order of his day put him to death,
The Temple Authorities wanted
things to stay the same,
as authorities are wont to do.

We're in huge trouble now, she said.
Change will occur no matter what we want.
We must consume less,
eat more rice and beans and less steak,
don't supersize our portions,
reduce our carbon footprint
give away more than just our excess.
We must change our lives.

We must preach the Gospel, too
this day and every day.
Use words, Saint Francis said,
if that is necessary.

Listening To The Silence

Suddenly the noise was gone.
No trucks barreling over Santiam Pass
on Highway 22, no revving Harleys
in the Pacific Crest Trailhead parking lot
or overheard camper conversations.

Nothing. Just silence in the air.
Three-Fingered Jack was five dusty miles ahead,
fourteen hundred feet uphill with thirty-seven-
pound packs. We anticipated all that but not
the ninety-three degree heat this cloudless day.

Now it was quiet. I could almost hear the air
move against itself. Sometimes it settled
on leaves lying at the side of the trail.
The hum of thousands of mosquitoes
came later when we emerged into the high

country by the lakes. The foot of snow blocking
the trail, two hundred fallen trees, and the bugs
were all ahead of us. Now all there was to do
was listen to the air circulating, watch
an ant cruising across a leaf, hear a poem.

I Knew Something Was Wrong

I knew something was wrong
when I pushed the accelerator
again and nothing happened.
The red dash lights flashed on,
the engine conked out, and the car
and I glided evenly to a stop
like a silk wrap settling
lovingly on bare shoulders.
I was stuck. In heavy traffic.
Two miles from the poetry reading.
This will be a challenge—finding
in this development a hidden good.

I Thought It Was Interesting

I thought it was interesting.
I gazed at a blank page in my poetry
notebook when we started to write.
The instructor, Peter Sears, gave us
directions: the poem must include a Z.
There, I did it already, like a contestant
on *What's My Line* getting his plug
on the air in the show's first minute.

I thought it was interesting
when the nurse unwrapped
the blood pressure cuff:
"Not bad today," she said.
I was expecting a much worse reading;
I was worried about the needle
piercing my vein any moment now.
After all, I was there by choice because
I thought it was the thing to do.

I was happy about that news
since I expected it to keep
being fine and the blood draw
went fine, actually, better than fine
but I knew one day, pointedly,
the news would be not so fine.
I'll have to work to be grateful for that
and that will be interesting.

*What's My Line? – *a quiz show in the 1950s.*

Arborvitae

After "Ask Me"
by William Stafford

Ask me what I would do if I could change the world
and I would tell you that's a dicey question.
Ask me if I have a plan about solving even a single
problem and I will tell you things take time.

Ask me if I think your gas station on Belvedere Avenue
will sell wind or light and I will tell you that maybe,
just maybe, we will invent chargers that condense
electricity or bag the wind. You and I can stare at the

oil train stretching a mile down the track, the last cars
out of sight around a curve, and know we need
to change our lives. Ask me how to proceed and I will
say we can gaze at the arborvitae swaying gracefully

in the wind. We know our future is rustling there.
Where the wind goes, that is where we will go.

ON THE FRONT PAGE OF THE *NEW YORK TIMES*

dateline Paris, Jan. 13, 2015

They were words, just words we could brush off
while getting to the next article about a failing

campaign for mayor or the latest Knicks loss,
brush off like the most recent Budweiser

commercial or the last replay on Sports Center.
They could be brushed off if it weren't for

that photo. My stomach went into freefall
like an elevator dropping fourteen stories; my heart

raced as if I were a condemned man walking
his last mile, as I glimpsed the picture snapped

a second before the black-hooded gunman emptied
the magazine of his AK-47 into the police officer

lying wounded on the cobblestoned pavement,
Rue de Rivoli, Paris, France. The officer

had raised his hand as if to ward off
the bullets that would shred it in a burst

of automatic weapon fire. The article at the right
of the picture read, "Terrorists strike Paris newspaper;

12 people killed," recounting the story of the surprise
midday attack. Was there a motive

for this action by these two hooded figures?
"Continued on Page A6," it read, and I turned

the sheets to find the reason for such slaughter.
There it was, on Page A6: someone had lampooned

Islam in a cartoon—for that offence, the black-hooded
figure pointed his killing stick nonchalantly

on the way by, just as in the movies, except
this time it would be, one second later, for real.

What to do, I thought. No easy answer came.
But I didn't read the rest of the paper, just the same.

BRAIN SURGERY

For Judith Barrington

i

She talked about herself in the third person,
her brain surgery and the clot in her frontal lobe,
how frightened she was and the mental

calisthenics she'd been doing for brain rehabilitation:
writing, puzzles, *New York Times* crosswords,
maybe a little Sudoku and tic-tac-toe on a napkin

like weight-lifting in the gym after hip surgery.
She talked about the doctors taking out pieces
of her brain and lamented losing three days.

Someone had asked her about them but she couldn't
remember; no matter what she did, three days had
disappeared from her life like in *The Lost Weekend*.

I saw the notice on Facebook for her reading,
the first one since her surgery nine months ago.
She seemed her old self, maybe better, as if she'd

never been away. Maybe it was relief, maybe the
comfort from a friendly crowd that wanted to hear
her, wanted her back and wouldn't judge her harshly.

ii

I could never write about my hip surgery
in any person, my second and third thoughts
about electing to have myself cut, checking myself

in, and how scared I was. A friend who had
the same surgery told me someone had
done a video of his surgery and posted it

on YouTube. I could go online and watch
everything that would happen to me. He did,
and was prepared, he said. I never did that.

All that receded when I saw how grateful she was
to be alive, to be back, able to read poetry.
I was inspired to write about my hidden truths.

Hat And House

My friend Paul was the first to raise
the question about my orange
Ascension Monastery hat
with the sunburst logo.
One day, the hat just wasn't there.
Searching didn't help; nor did waiting
for it to turn up in an unlikely place.
All of a sudden it was gone.
I assumed it was just carelessness
but really somebody could have stolen it.
I can order a replacement any day
but still look for it when I go to the hat rack.

That question was like my Tudor-style
house. One day it wasn't there either.
I know where it is, however, but
thought the two were similar.
I actually planned losing my house,
thought it was the right thing to sell it.
I realized the difference only later,
Living in a smaller, nondescript house.
I learned you can't go back
even though you think it's possible.
That was a different kind of carelessness.

Reel To Reel

You don't have much to say these
days, my treasured relic from earlier
times, before the long night of the compact
disc thudded into its dominate position,
pushed you to the sidelines, a substitute
who never recovers from an ACL* tear,
no matter how much the rehabilitation.

You had occupied a two-foot-long space
on my music shelf, the prominent member,
till your nephew, the cassette tape deck,
smaller, easier, narrower, slipped in. Your
shiny reels would turn quietly, ever so quietly,
producing, it's hard to believe now, an
hour and a half of uninterrupted delights

like musical magnolias blooming
in nightly moon shadow. I remember
the day our modern stereo receiver,
sporting only two plugs for tape decks,
arrived by Fed-Ex Special Delivery.
Your younger cousin, the compact disc
player, supplanted you.

There was no funeral.
There were no commemorations,
no second act, as Scott Fitzgerald said,
only a fast descent to an already
over-crowded basement. Today your green,
boxed tapes are packed in cupboards;
you sit in your hard, brown case, praying,
like vinyl, for a return to the spotlight.

*ACL—The anterior **cruciate ligament**
is one of the four major ligaments of the human knee.*

Evening Encounter

You speak only when spoken to,
sitting upright on the sumptuous couch,
hair trimmed neatly around your head

in the same tight package as the whole person.
"Things are nice at the beach," you say,
you're seeing him tomorrow, "as a friend."

You hope he doesn't expect more.
"Your book is good reading," you say,
you're dating someone at the coast.

You talk about your interests, and your eyes
continually return to your book.
"I must prepare for my book group," you say.

No questions, no comments, no conversation,
the evening encounter at an end. The light
remains medium, and Chopin fills the room.

A Case Of Tax Reform

I squirmed through the December 4 article
in the *New York Times* about the proposed tax bill.

The Senate had passed it late the night before
without debate. I'd become increasingly

worried about this developing tax change.
They call it "tax reform," but I didn't see any

"reform" in it, only a continual drift of money
from our family and all the families like us

to the ultra-rich and the corporations. I read
Paul Ryan, the House Speaker's, comments

about it, how this reform would, to hear him
tell it, benefit almost everybody. I was baffled

because he is Catholic, a Catholic who knows
about the Pharisees, knows that they laid burdens

on the people, knows the story of the Good Samaritan,
and still is willing to cut people off Medicaid,

willing to have their health insurance costs increase,
if they can get health insurance, willing for them

to pay more taxes so the President and the
Republicans can have a big "win." I listen

to the Speaker talk but can never discern whether
he understands any of the results of his, and his party's,

actions. My wife and I could get by on one less
dinner out, one less paper a week, fewer nasal

decongestants for her vertigo. We both received
"cost of living" increases in our pension and

Social Security checks. But the lady living
in subsidized housing to whom we took

a food basket this morning, this lady who had
to take a cab to the veterinary hospital to get

treatment for her dog, this lady can't pay more
taxes, can't afford more medical care, doesn't

know where her next meal, her next cab fare,
or her dog's next rabies shots are coming from.

I remember the Roman Plebeians in the time of
Coriolanus* starving while the patricians hoarded

food, the Plebeians who decided violence
was the only solution, who revolted when they

saw that the people living in their villas at the top
didn't care whether the people below lived or died.

Is this what is happening to our country today?
No, people wouldn't come to that same conclusion.

Coriolanus
A Roman patrician in the early days
of the Republic, and the subject of one of
Shakespeare's later plays.

Yellow

Yellow is an attitude, the dust
on the piano and nostalgia
for the dawn. It is a lion cub
sunning himself on the veldt,
bananas, and the splash of lemon
juice at Harry's Bar in Havana.
It is English in the morning, a
single salmon squash at the picnic,
a lone rider approaching Samarra.

Yellow is happy in the early morning
hours, hopeful, kind, a blast of
Good Morning America.
It is the Yellow Submarine
running on rechargeable batteries.
It is a bird on the wire above
the Amazon. It is love in the
evening before the blue-dark of night
slips in over Mt. Jefferson.

Yellow is a mercurial friend,
solid at nine AM, squishy in
the afternoon, fading in the evening.
It is a placeholder, a tart smell of
lemon, a passion flower in the sweat
of the sunset. It is a 1995 Subaru Loyale
four-door sedan, custom edition; it is
a candidate for the Supreme Court
vacancy with a 190 IQ. It is my life.

Midnight Mass

Tonight Midnight Mass is at 10:30
but I still call it Midnight Mass.
I explained that to my daughter and
granddaughter, hoping they would come.
"And carols are at 9:45," I said.

They don't remember when it was actually
at midnight as when I was a kid,
and in Latin, ending at two in the morning.
We went home after that to open
presents, getting to bed before dawn.

Later I became aware how much
my parents indulged me,
staying up because it was important
to a ten-year-old.

I remember loving it.
It was what we did.
It was the way things were and
I opened two presents.
Any tiredness we felt has faded
into the mist of memory,
like Humphrey Bogart walking off
into the fog at the end of *Casablanca.*

I don't even remember any problems,
only the fun of *finally*
getting to open presents
after waiting
all that time through Mass.

That's what I told my daughter
and granddaughter,

but that was too late for them,
whether the Mass was in Latin
or in English,
whether at midnight or 10:30.
But I still like it.
I still call it Midnight Mass
even though it's at 10:30 PM.

Time For Biff

I heard the soft voice whisper about my friend
Biff in the adult care facility: "Let it out, put it

down, be there now," pulling me through this white
desert of anger, this blue melancholy of loss.

I remember the fun times when we were young,
listening to the Top 91 on New Year's Eve,

partying at Chico's Pizza on Saturday night,
playing bridge in college and into our adult lives.

But then one day I looked and found a hole—
you were gone—where, I didn't know.

Was it my job to break through your defenses
when you resisted in every way you could?

We called you "eccentric," and maybe that was it,
a name we put on something we couldn't understand.

Wasn't respecting your wishes the right thing to do?
Then one day in the care facility after your stroke

you told me yourself: "If I don't want to do something,
I just don't do it." A light clicked on in my brain,

illuminating as a flashlight switched on in a pitch dark
cave. I understood why you didn't develop your dazzling

speed in high school, why you refused physical therapy,
how you became a difficult patient, why you could

retreat so easily into inactivity. How brazen you were
to follow that dark muse, no matter the fearful cost.

Hospital Room

We sat by your bed in the River Bend Hospital,
a calming picture overhead as the nurses started

unhooking your tubes. I heard the doctor say
there was nothing more they could do today,

"He was probably dead when he arrived in the ER."
I held your hand and it was still warm, lying above

blood on the white sheet, a tube still in your throat,
hoses in both nostrils. We said the "Our Father."

I was holding your hand and had this crystal impression,
this sudden notion that you would rise up off the bed

just as in the movies in response to our prayer. You
looked as though you could do it, had the willpower.

I remembered my confidence on the drive
down from Milwaukie that you would be okay.

"People have heart attacks and recover every day."
I was convinced of it.

But nothing happened.
You kept lying there and my expectations drained

like a slow leak from a bicycle tire, an epic erosion
as reality set in; you weren't going to get up.

I needed to hold your hand for a long time,
till it grew cold, acknowledging your passing.

GRATITUDE

After "Celebration"
by Grace Schulman

I thought of goslings swimming in Benson Lake,
magnolia petals lying amid the tall April grass

uncut since October, clover
and pink rhododendrons, pungent dandelion

juice dribbling down transparent stalks,
water lapping on the bank with

geese honking in a feeding frenzy.
Snow still covers the high country till July.

How is it possible to be sufficiently grateful
for my reconstructed heart?

I mourn for days irretrievably lost in the past,
the inability to walk around the lake today,

the energy that used to flow unencumbered,
the endless trips to the bathroom,

the need to lift nothing heavier than five
pounds. How can I be grateful enough

for the loss of the burning in my chest
every time I took a walk,

the angina that flared like a screeching hawk?
They tell me all will be well,

better than before,
like the aroma of mint leaves in summer tea.

How can I be grateful enough for
continued shelter under your hovering wings?

I can almost hear them fluttering,
like the growth of new spring grass.

Yellow Bird Is Happy

The yellow bird looked happy today
perched on the wooden deck railing,
pleased with the birdseed evenly laid out.

Usually he was too shy to come first to eat,
waiting till after the loud-mouthed
red birds ate their fill. The green birds

usually didn't get up this early, they were
no problem and the black birds were nesting
by the lake. Today he'd read a little before

rising, his latest book *Bird Watchers: Their
Habits and Neuroses*. Why anyone would
travel miles to sit, he thought, in a stinking bog

to watch what birds did and write their names
down in a sodden notebook was beyond him.
But today he let all that go. He even thought

he was getting a little sunburn, which would help
his feelings of inferiority. Today he was happy
to be alive, to be who and where he was, unlike

the red bird who always wanted to be someone else,
the green bird that was always looking for harmony,
or the black bird who was always flying away.

He watched *She Wore a Yellow Ribbon* last night,
then had a nightmare about turning red for a day,
waking up before he knew the ending.

Today he liked being yellow, being alive, healthy,
basking in the translucent sunlight of summer,
for today, not wanting to be different anymore.

The Invisible Boundary

She knew immediately they were there.
She never should have ventured
outside the National Park boundary.

She wasn't sure how she knew
but she hadn't gone twenty-five
paces in that avocado spring day

before the nut-brown hairs on
the back of her neck stood straight.
It was just a feeling she had at first.

Then she heard a twig quietly snap
as if the presence wanted desperately
to disguise getting into position.

But she heard the click. She knew he
was facing her. There was only the vision
of a metal gun barrel behind faded vegetation.

She never saw anything — no shadow,
no face, no trigger, no bullet.
It was only her spring sense that

moved her to jump sideways into
the pea-green bushes as she heard
the crack sail into the pale poplar.

Into the brush she darted, back the way
she came into the green forest, part the
imaginary boundary line, to sanctuary.

The Oatfield House

In 1910, the road was dirt in the summer,
mud in the winter. An occasional new
Model T raced along toward Oregon City.
But mostly wagons and horses moved folks

up here on the hill, above the interurban
streetcar on McLoughlin. Or they walked.
Horses did their business in the road, nobody
to shovel it up as they do now in a parade.

Today the road is solid blacktop, yellow
stripe in the middle, white lines on the sides
for the bike lanes, ambulances and police
cars, Tri-Met buses cruising past incessantly

in each direction belching gray fumes like
runaway stagecoaches to Lordsburg or
Aurora. Waves of automobiles and trucks
roll at rush hours, narrowly avoiding runners

on the sides of the road. To avoid the traffic,
squirrels scamper along telephone wires
stretching across the street. Occasionally one falls
or is knocked off, becoming crow food. Houses

are closer, manicured yards mowed by electric
tractors and gas-powered yard trimmers,
pollsters calling day and night to get opinions.
If they ask for Thomas, he's never home.

The entrance today is in the front, not on the
south side. A garage sits there, arborvitae
and a lamppost frame the yard, a deck and
hot tub rest behind the house to the west.

A garden and rose bushes divide the yard,
pampas grass leaning into the wind.
Today the house lives its renewed life,
a jewel tucked into growing suburbia.

Facing The Equinox

Spring smiles just past next Sunday,
its milepost driven into the solid earth.

Days lengthen and the hope of exciting
adventures rests in the days to come.

My expectations rise as the days stretch,
sunrise a few minutes earlier each day,

sunset several ticks later each evening.
This is my happiest time of the year

with these longer days and shorter nights.
After the Equinox, spring will be truly here,

even though we don't notice it till we're hiking
one evening and the sun is still out at 9 PM.

Tree House

I saw a tree house today while
walking with my granddaughter
Emma along Meadowlark Lane
strewn with cherry blossoms
crying out like gossamer gumdrops
on the slippery spring pavement.

It was a complete building finished
with a corrugated roof and boards
covering windows looking like
cannon ports on a Ship o' the Line
to keep out any unwanted intruder.
Two ladders rose to the house

and even though they were side-by-
side, one looked every bit an entrance,
the other like a last-ditch escape hatch
from prying parents or space invaders.
I'd walked this street a hundred times
before, but, as things would be with

tree houses and purloined letters
in plain view, never saw this dwelling
till this instant; when I was walking,
slowed down, with my granddaughter,
paying attention to things like tree houses.
It seemed to shout "see me" today.

The Three Essentials

One night in camp on the Pacific Crest Trail
just over the border into Northern California
I heard the soft whisper, "Pump, Pack, Pray."

These are the three essentials. You must guard
your filter, pump your water, carry it with you;
otherwise, you can't go on more than a day.

You must pack your equipment for your time
in the wilderness, otherwise, you'll be very cold
when it's dark and you've forgotten your tent.

Most important of all is to pray. It's third
in this poem, a place of honor. The spirit
called me to put it there. Otherwise, I would

have been hiking a three-thousand-foot
rocky decline alone with evil perched over
my right shoulder and a drop-off to the left.

I heard the whisper: "pump, pack, pray."

About The Author

Tom Hogan was born in Portland, Oregon, and raised in the Portland area. He is the author of five chapbooks of poetry: *Poems for the Journey* (2001), *Main Roads and Byways* (2005), *Texas Dawning* (Fir Tree Press, 2006), *Clouds and Water* (Fir Tree Press, 2007), and *Cathedral Rock* (Fir Tree Press, 2008).

His first book of poetry, *The Promise of the Trail,* was published by Dancing Moon Press in October 2014. This new book, *Giving Thanks: New and Selected Poems*, was published by Dancing Moon Press as well, in 2018.

He directs the Milwaukie Poetry Series in Milwaukie, Oregon, currently in its twelfth season.

As well as writing, Tom is trained as a Social Worker and has a part-time private practice as an LCSW. He has a B.A. in Liberal Arts from the University of Portland (1964), an M.A. in history from the University of Oregon (1966), and an M.S.W. from Portland State University (1969).

Tom is a hiker and backpacker and has been working on the Pacific Crest Trail, among other destinations, for some time. He finished hiking the Oregon portion of the trail, and has five sections left in Washington.

He has a daughter, Lisa, a granddaughter, Emma, and a stepdaughter, Alli. He lives with his wife, Jane, and their two cats, in Milwaukie, Oregon.